"No man has influenced me more through his teaching and example than Major Ian Thomas. And no teaching has been more foundational in my life and ministry than his powerful exposition of the indwelling life of the risen Christ."

D. STUART BRISCOE
MINISTER-AT-LARGE, ELMBROOK CHURCH

"True repentance says, 'I can't,' and true faith says, 'Christ can.' We cannot live the Christian life on our own or by our own strength, and Jesus says, 'I never said you could. I always said I would.' Those were powerful, sweet words to me as a thirteen-year-old boy listening to Ian Thomas in 1949, and they are still powerfully true. Life in Christ is a most exciting adventure, so hang on! Let Jesus do it, and say thank you to Him every day for what He will do in and through you. *The Indwelling Life of Christ* will enable you to get there."

RT. REV. DR. TERENCE KELSHAW
BISHOP, DIOCESE OF THE RIO GRANDE

"Through failure and discouragement, Ian Thomas discovered at a young age that he could not live the Christian life—only Christ could live it in him, through him. He has shared this timeless truth for six decades on every continent, to the immense enrichment and transformation of countless people. He speaks again to a new generation in this book, which will stimulate your mind, warm your heart, and draw your will to rest in the sufficiency of the Life indwelling every believer—the actual life of Christ Himself."

CHARLES PRICE
SENIOR PASTOR, THE PEOPLE'S CHURCH
TORONTO, ONTARIO

The
Indwelling
LIFE *of*
CHRIST

MAJOR
W. IAN THOMAS

Multnomah Books

THE INDWELLING LIFE OF CHRIST
published by Multnomah Books

© 2006 by Major Ian Thomas
International Standard Book Number: 978-1-59052-524-1

Cover image by Scott Tysick/Masterfile

Italics in Scripture quotations are the author's emphasis.
Unless otherwise indicated, Scripture quotations are from:
The Holy Bible, New King James Version
© 1984 by Thomas Nelson, Inc.
Other Scripture quotations are from:
The Amplified Bible (AMP)
© 1965, 1987 by Zondervan Publishing House.
The Amplified New Testament © 1958, 1987 by the Lockman Foundation.
The Holy Bible, King James Version (KJV)
Holy Bible, New Living Translation (NLT)
© 1996. Used by permission of Tyndale House Publishers, Inc.
All rights reserved.

Published in the United States by WaterBrook Multnomah, an imprint of the Crown Publishing
Group, a division of Random House Inc., New York.

MULTNOMAH and its mountain colophon are registered trademarks of Random House Inc.

Printed in the United States of America

For information:
MULTNOMAH BOOKS
12265 ORACLE BOULEVARD, SUITE 200
COLORADO SPRINGS, CO 80921

Library of Congress Cataloging-in-Publication Data

Thomas, W. Ian.
  The indwelling life of Christ / W. Ian Thomas.
    p. cm.
  ISBN 1-59052-524-8
  1. Christian life. I. Title.
  BV4501.3.T472 2006
  248.4--dc22

                              2005026805

                        11—10 9

CONTENTS

Rediscovering Jesus

To be entirely honest, I know of nothing quite so boring as Christianity without Christ.

Countless people have stopped going to a place of worship simply because they are sick of going through the motions of a dead religion. They are tired of trying to start a car on an empty tank. What a pity that there are not more people around to show them that Jesus Christ is *alive*.

I know of nothing so utterly exciting as being a Christian, sharing the very Life of Jesus Christ on earth right here and now, being caught up with Him into the relentless, invincible purposes of the almighty God, and having available to us all the limitless resources of Deity for accomplishing those purposes.

Can you imagine anything more exciting than that?

PROFOUND SIMPLICITY

Every week I receive letters from people who know that excitement, and who, in one way or another, have been exposed in the past to the ministry I have been a part of now for more than seventy years. These are people who have participated in one of our conferences or read one of our books or listened to a tape. They contact me to explain what happened to them when finally, in the gracious revelation that the Holy Spirit delights to give, they rediscover Jesus.

It does not happen all at once. At first they are often a bit bewildered by what they hear, and it seems to go right over their head. Then slowly, bit by bit, there is that revelation and then a moment of truth. It becomes so clear, so divinely obvious. So completely logical. Profoundly simple and simply profound.

This profound simplicity is something Paul spoke of in his second epistle to the Corinthians. His readers were those who knew Christ as their Redeemer. They were born again, their names were written in the Lamb's Book of Life, and they were heavenbound, yet Paul had a grave concern for them: "I fear, lest somehow, as the serpent deceived Eve by his craftiness, so your minds may be corrupted from *the simplicity that is in Christ*" (2 Corinthians 11:3).

Paul was anxiously concerned that nothing in their lives would detract from the sheer simplicity which is in Christ, the centrality of a *Person,* the Lord Jesus Himself, in residence within their redeemed humanity.

OUR GREATEST NEED

Experiencing this simplicity is the greatest need today throughout the Church worldwide. The utmost need in every ministry group, every missionary outreach, every denomination, is to *rediscover the Lord Jesus Christ* and the indispensability of His indwelling presence within the believer. This means encountering the risen living Lord who shares His Life with us on earth on our way to heaven…so that He may accomplish *through us* what He began to do in His own physical body two thousand years ago.

What a fantastic privilege!

To help move us toward that rediscovery and that privilege, in this book we will focus continually on the Lord Jesus, because only Christ is capable of living the Christian life, for the very obvious and simple reason that He *is* the Christian life. We will look to Him to learn how He lived *as Man* in His relationship to the Father when He came to live upon this earth. He will show us how He intends us to live in our relationship to Him, helping us discover in fuller depth what it means not just to become a Christian but actually to *be* one, and giving us a new vision for all that being a Christian really means.

A PURPOSEFUL CHRISTIAN LIFE

Do you know what it is to live purposefully? Is there an urgent sense of mission or some compelling thrust within you which makes life add up to the sheer adventure that God always intended life to be?

Or are you simply engaged in the struggle for existence and survival?

Worse still, have you been caught up into the rat race of competitive existence? Haunted by the fear of being overtaken by others at the next bend in the road? Breathlessly trying to keep up with events that travel faster than your capacity to cope with them?

If so, there is good news awaiting you, good news about a treasury of purpose and truth and wisdom to be found in the person of Christ, for living purposefully means trading our poverty for Christ's wealth...our weakness for Christ's strength. We exchange the bankruptcy of the fallen Adam for all the fullness of the Life of Christ, and we discover the sheer adventure of allowing Jesus Christ to *be God* in our own experience, for God He is!

That is why detaching your Christianity from Christ is to reduce it to the impotence of a dead religion, impersonal to Him and impersonal to you, just an intellectual exercise or a sentimental formula—and Christianity is neither.

Christianity is *Christ*. It involves a principle of life which pulsates with divine energy and cannot be explained apart from God Himself. It is essentially miraculous even though it does not have to be sensational. It is always supernatural, lying beyond the scope of mortal man, apart from the indwelling presence of the risen Son of God.

Just as Jesus acted in the sinless humanity which the Father had prepared for Him in the thirty-three years of His life on earth, so He wants to behave in *your* humanity presented to Him now. The Christian life is nothing less than the life which He lived then...lived *now* by Him in *you*.

The Indwelling
LIFE *of*
CHRIST

ABOUT THIS BOOK

A brief word about this book's format: You will find fifty individual readings here, all of them short. I encourage you, however, to read just one each day—allowing yourself to linger reflectively on each one.

After each reading you will find a few questions for your reflection and application. Take time to think carefully about these, to help you act on what you learn and become convinced of—for only then will you experience the liberating power of the truth.

1

Finding God on Earth

Imagine that far out in space, in another galaxy, there is a planet inhabited by intelligent creatures. These creatures and their planet and galaxy were of course fashioned by the God who created everything. But they do not know what God is like, though they possess an insatiable appetite to find out more about Him.

Then one day they detect, through their highly developed forms of intergalactic surveillance, the existence of a planet called Earth. They also make initial discoveries about the human beings who dwell there. Immediately, and with intense excitement, they mobilize their resources to build a spaceship capable of sending a delegation to faraway Earth with the specific goal of going there to learn about God.

Why Earth? Because their initial findings have disclosed the record of what God said when He first created human beings on this planet—that He was making them in His own image and according to His own likeness. Such a revelation is absolutely the most thrilling news these alien beings have ever heard. By getting a close-up view of humanity, they will be getting their first-ever glimpse of God.

With the spaceship completed and a carefully chosen delegation ready to embark, great crowds gather to see them off and wish them well.

After a long voyage across several galaxies, the hearts of every member of this delegation beat faster as Earth comes into view. This beautiful blue planet grows larger and larger as they come closer. "Soon we will see man," they tell each other, "the creature God made in His perfect image. We will be able to return home with eyewitness knowledge and understanding of what God is really like."

Slowly and softly their spacecraft makes its landing on Earth…and the alien creatures step out.

They have landed on a vacant lot in a city (much like whatever city you know best). They leave their spacecraft and walk down the nearest street. The first human being they lay eyes upon is a body sprawled on the curb that they have to step over, a drunk (though the aliens do not know about drunkenness) who is lying there in his own vomit. The aliens try talking to him, but the man only moans and rolls over.

Leaving the drunk behind, they turn a corner and suddenly confront two rival groups of young men threatening each other with knives. They have scarred arms and a lifeless stare in their eyes (though the aliens have not learned about drug abuse).

Stunned by this unexpected danger, the aliens turn quickly in a different direction and hear sounds from an open door under a tavern sign, and they enter the safety inside. The few people there ignore them. They have sullen faces as they sit in booths at the room's shadowy edges.

The sound the aliens were hearing is coming from a television set above the bar, and on the screen someone is announcing the "world news." The aliens crowd closer to catch a summary of what is happening all around this Earth. The "news" they hear is about terrorist bombers and murderers. It is about corruption in business and government. It is about childish and foolish behavior by celebrities in the realms of entertainment and sports.

The aliens stare in shock at the screen, until one of them turns to the others and says, "Let's get off this planet. This place stinks."

With heavy steps they make their way to the spaceship, weighed down by revulsion and disillusionment over this display of God's character. And on their long, sad journey back, they wrestle with their total loss at knowing how to convey this tragic discovery to their loved ones at home.

Of course, you and I know that what they actually learned was not what God is like, but what sin is like. Was there anything wrong, however, in the logic behind their expectation of seeing God on our planet?

No, their thinking was entirely correct, as we see more clearly when we carefully read the Scriptures.

In the day that God created man, He made him in the likeness of God.... In the image of God He made man.

GENESIS 5:1; 9:6

→ What does it fully mean to you that you have been created in God's image and likeness?

→ What things should logically be expected from someone who is made in God's image and likeness?

2

Are You Normal?

re you normal? You would probably answer yes to that question, but do you really know what normality is for a human being?

After all, a knowledge of normality is the only basis upon which we can diagnose accurately. That is why we have to understand very clearly how God created us; only then can we have an intelligent understanding of what has gone wrong, and its consequences, and what God has done to put things right.

In Psalm 8, David asks God, *"What is man* that You are mindful of him?" Then David acknowledges, "You have made him a little lower than the angels, and You have crowned him with glory and honor. You have made him to have dominion over the works of Your hands; You have put all things under his feet" (Psalm 8:4–6). This was man in his innocence, man in normality, man as God created him in Adam: *crowned with glory!*

What was the glory with which God crowned man? God had said, "Let Us make man in Our image, according to Our likeness" (Genesis 1:26). Man in the image of God was to be equipped by His divine indwelling, the Holy Spirit occupying the human spirit, so that man would manifest the very glory of God. It was a *derived* glory, exclusively dependent upon the presence of the Creator within the creature. Likewise the authority man was to exercise over the earth was the authority that derived exclusively from his submission to God's authority.

The Bible makes it abundantly clear that God Himself (the Creator within the creature) must be the origin of His own image. After God completed His work of creation by creating man, "God saw everything that He had made, and indeed it was very good" (Genesis 1:31). What did He see in that moment when He looked at man whom He created in His perfect image? He saw *Himself!* For "God created man in His own image; in the image of God He created him" (Genesis 1:27).

God Himself, as our Creator, always intended that He should indwell us; His cherished ambition was to be seen and heard in those He created. *That* is normality for a human being, when God Himself is behaving in and through a man or woman. This is the purpose for which He created us, that we might be a physical, visible expression on this earth of the

God who is otherwise invisible, as John tells us: "No one has seen God at any time" (John 1:18).

God created each human being with a physical, visible, and audible body to be inhabited by an invisible God, to make Himself visible through what that person does and says and is. God Himself must be the origin of this activity within us, which is called *righteousness*. God is the author of all righteousness, and for you and me to produce it, He must be within us the origin of His own image, the source of His own activity, the dynamic of His own demands, and the cause of His own effect.

Therefore if any human being is truly normal in his or her behavior, there is only One Person to be congratulated, and that is God Himself. Normality for a human being is when God can be seen by anything and everything which that person does and says and is.

Our "natural" man, or who we are in our flesh, is void of righteousness and also of any true spirituality: "The natural man does not receive the things of the Spirit of God, for they are foolishness to him; nor can he know them, because they are spiritually discerned" (1 Corinthians 2:14). The natural man cannot know the things of the Spirit of God because he is morally and intellectually incapacitated. The natural man is not normal; he is *not* what God created and intended man to be. In his fallen condition he is destitute, empty, and alienated from the person of his Creator.

The moment you come to realize that only God can make a person righteous and godly, you are left with no option but to *find* God, and to *know* Him, and to let God be

God in and through you, whatever that will mean. This will leave you with no margin for picking and choosing, for there is only one God, and He is absolute, and He made you expressly for Himself.

> *Be renewed in the spirit of your mind,*
> *and...put on the new man which*
> *was created according to God,*
> *in true righteousness and holiness.*
>
> EPHESIANS 4:23–24

+ How normal are you? What is true normality for a human being?

+ What does it mean "to let God be God in and through you"?

3

The One Indispensability for Our Humanity

n oil lamp needs oil to produce light. Why? Because the lamp was made to function in that way. A car needs gasoline to go. Why? Because the car was made to function in that way.

Why does a human being need God to be functional? Because we were made that way. Long ago, God decided to make a creature on this little planet called Earth. He specifically designed this creature as the means whereby His potential, His Life, could be released and produce righteousness.

Man cannot produce righteousness on his own, however, any more than a car can go or an oil lamp can shine without fuel.

Trying to light an oil lamp with no oil is illogical and useless; you will remain in the dark. Trying to drive your car without gasoline is likewise utterly unreasonable; you will end up by getting out and pushing it, going only as far and fast as your physical strength allows, and bringing yourself to exhaustion.

The same is true with human beings. Simply urging them to be good, telling them to draw from the depths of their personality, introducing them to behavioral science, trying to legislate their actions with rules, regulations, and religion, and threatening them with punishment or prison— ultimately none of these can succeed in producing righteousness from human beings.

To get light from an oil lamp, filling it first with oil is entirely reasonable. To get a car to provide you with transportation, filling the tank with gas is completely logical. In the same way, divine logic affirms that obtaining righteousness from a man or woman happens only when that person is filled with God. Oil in the lamp, gas in the car…and Christ in the Christian. It takes God to be a man, and that is why it takes Christ to be a Christian, because Christ puts God back into a man, the only way we can again become functional.

It is called the new birth, being born again, as our soul is awakened by God's Spirit. It can happen only on God's terms, and it restores us to that for which God created us—of being functional only by virtue of His presence within us. God is indispensable for the truly normal human being.

Man was created uniquely, in such a way that he can enjoy a moral relationship between the creature and his Creator, because God is love, and the only thing that satisfies love is to be loved. The only thing that satisfies friendship is to be befriended.

Love and friendship cannot be forced, however. If God wanted a man who could love Him back, that man could not be like any other creature, without any moral capacity either to please God or displease Him. Such a creature would be amoral, doing what it does because it must, rather than evidencing any disposition toward his Maker.

You and I, however, were so created that by anything and everything we do, we are saying to our Creator either "God, I love you," or "God, I could not care less."

The human spirit is that part of us where God lives within us in the person of the Holy Spirit, so that with our moral consent (and never without it), God gains access to our human soul. This is where He Himself, as the Creator within the creature, can teach our minds, control our emotions, and direct our wills, so that He, as God from within, governs our behavior as we let God be God.

"If we live in the Spirit, let us also walk in the Spirit" (Galatians 5:25), and this is what it means to walk in the Holy Spirit: to take one step at a time, and for every new situation into which every new step takes you, no matter what it may be, to hear Christ saying to your heart, "I AM," then to look up into His face by faith and say, *"You are!* That is all I need to know, Lord, and I thank You, for You are never less than adequate."

The LORD is the strength of my life.

PSALM 27:1

→ How have you recognized your need for God in daily life?

→ In what you say and do, how are you saying to your Creator either "God, I love you," or "God, I could not care less"?

4

Instinct for Animals, the Holy Spirit for Man

God created every human being with a body, a physical form. This is something we share with all forms of created life on earth, with animals as well as plants. God also gave every human being the capacity to think, react, and decide—mind, emotion, and will. We can group these psychological behavior mechanisms and think of them together as the *soul*. It is within the soul that human behavior is determined, for it is here where decisions are made, plans are conceived, and the will is exercised to bring the body into action. The will is exercised under the influence of the mind and the emotions; whatever influence controls our mind and emotions will ultimately control our will. Through the behavior that results from this active operation of our soul, the thoughts and intents of our heart are communicated to the outside world.

The soul as so defined is a characteristic that we share with animals, but not with plants. It may surprise you to think of animals as having souls—minds to think with, emotions to react with, and wills to decide with. If so, here is a simple experiment you can try: Find a stick, then find a wasps' nest and poke it with the stick. You will discover that wasps have a highly developed emotional capacity: They can get very angry. You will also see that wasps have a highly developed intellectual capacity to determine exactly who is stirring up their nest. Not only that, but you will find they have a highly developed volitional capacity, a will to wreak vengeance on their enemy. Though by that time, in all probability, you will not be hanging around to find out anything more.

So animals are like human beings in that they have a soul, a capacity to think, react, and decide. God however did not create animals with the capacity to be inhabited by their Creator, as man was. Instead, God built into animals a unique and wonderful mechanism called *instinct*. This is the indispensable means by which He protects them and governs their behavior.

Because of instinct, the behavior patterns of animals are

repetitive and predictable, but there is no moral relationship between the animals and their Creator, as there is between human beings and God. Every bird or beast or insect does what it does because it *must*. It is governed by a law of compulsion that operates in the soul of every animal to teach its mind, control its emotions, and direct its will.

Instinct is indispensable to animals in the same way that the Holy Spirit is indispensable to us in our humanity. Human beings are uniquely made with the capacity to be governed by God Himself dwelling within the human spirit in intimate identity with the human soul, so that God, within the human spirit, gains access to the human soul. There He plays that role in man's soul which instinct plays in the animal—teaching the mind, controlling the emotions, and directing the will. In this way, according to His intended design and purpose, He governs our behavior, so that He in us is the origin of His own image, source of His own activity, dynamic of His own demands, and cause of His own effect.

God has created us to be functional only by virtue of His presence, exercising His divine sovereignty within our humanity so that out of our love for Him, we live in utter dependence upon Him. Moreover, the only evidence any of us can give of such dependence on Him is our unquestioning obedience to Him.

That is the threefold moral relationship—love for Him, dependence upon Him, and obedience to Him—that allows God to *be* God in action within a human being.

This is also the threefold moral relationship which Jesus Christ, for thirty-three years on earth, expressed toward His Father. His love for the Father demanded absolute, unquestioning dependence upon the Father and total obedience to the Father. That is why He said that without His Father, He could do nothing (John 5:19, 30). The true sinlessness of Jesus was His constant reliance on the Father, never falling back on Himself.

If you and I are to be functional, this same relationship that existed between Jesus Christ and His Father in heaven must also be the relationship between ourselves and the Lord Jesus.

None of us are essential to God, but He is essentially indispensable to each of us. God so engineered you and me that His presence is indispensable to our humanity, teaching our minds, controlling our emotions, directing our wills, and governing our behavior.

Your new birth puts God into action *in you.* It lets all of God loose, clothed with the redeemed humanity of your own flesh and blood as a forgiven sinner, so that at last you become a normal human being as Jesus was.

God is able to make all grace abound toward you, that you, always having all sufficiency in all things, may have an abundance for every good work.

2 CORINTHIANS 9:8

- How are you letting all of God loose in your life?

- How are you allowing God at this time to teach your
  mind, control your emotions, direct your will, and govern your behavior?

5

God's Reasonable Demands

From God's point of view, every demand He makes of us is completely logical. Only from our fallen human point of view is it utterly unreasonable.

What does God demand of us?

In the final verse of Matthew 5, Jesus says, "You shall be perfect…" Reading that, we may get a little hot under the collar and ask, *"How* perfect?"

Jesus answers, "…just as your Father in heaven is perfect" (Matthew 5:48). In other words, when you are as perfect as the Father in heaven, you are okay. When others can look at you and actually see what God is like, you are all right.

Any complaints? Is there any reason why a God who created us in His own perfect, absolute likeness and image should not have the right to expect anything less than perfection from you and me? Is there any logical reason why He should *not* demand that?

None whatsoever!

Such a demand seems unreasonable to fallen man only because in the divine logic there is a hidden factor which is absent in the human reason of a fallen race. That hidden factor, in all its sublime simplicity, is God Himself. He so engineered us that the presence of the Creator within the creature is indispensable to our humanity.

When God made you and me, His intention was that we in normality would be distinguishable from the animal kingdom by a quality of life and behavior that would allow for absolutely no possible explanation but *God within us*.

God's written Word fully establishes this standard of behavior. At Mount Sinai, God gave Moses that which we call the Ten Commandments, or the moral law. What is the substance of this moral law?

Well, among other things, "Do not lie." You might respond, "Why not lie? Sometimes lying gets me out of trouble. Was God's law given simply to make my life difficult?"

No, the law was given simply that you and I might know what the Holy God demands from the human beings He created to advertise His Deity. So when the law states, "Do not lie," God is simply saying, "You were made to reflect My glory as God, and I am not a liar."

When God's law says, "Do not steal," He is telling us, "I created you in My image so that all creation can look at you and know what God is like, and I am not a thief."

His law states, "Do not commit adultery." He is simply saying, "You are a creature to whom I have given a body to express the fact that your physical and visible form is inhabited and governed by the God who is Spirit and invisible. I designed it this way so that everyone, by looking at your behavior, will know how I Myself behave, and I am not an adulterer; I do not indulge in promiscuous sex."

Now that is the law. It simply represents the minimal demands of a holy God, who has the absolute right to make those demands of those He created for the very purpose of revealing His character.

These demands and the kind of life they reflect are called in Scripture "the righteousness *of God*" (Romans 3:21–22; 10:3; 2 Corinthians 5:21), for it is the action of *God Himself.* There is no other righteousness on our part that God recognizes—only His own.

> *God is light and in Him is*
> *no darkness at all.*
> 1 JOHN 1:5

→ What commands from God's Word have you sometimes tended to view as unreasonable? How can you see,
  from God's point of view, that it is actually a logical and
  reasonable expectation?

→ What is true righteousness, from God's point of view?

6

When Doing Right Is Wrong

In the wilderness, Moses commanded the people of
Israel, "You shall not at all do as we are doing here
today—every man doing whatever is right..."
(Deuteronomy 12:8).

Why was he telling them not to continue doing what was
right? Doing right is what we are always supposed to do, is it
not?

Listen to Moses' words in full: "You shall not at all do as
we are doing here today—every man doing *whatever is right
in his own eyes.*"

The people were doing only what was right in their own eyes, without consulting the One who alone has the right to decide what is right and wrong.

This continues to be the curse of God's people today. We fail to seek counsel from the One who alone is King in His kingdom, and who alone has the right to call the shots.

Why were God's people in the wilderness unable to discern what was truly right? Moses goes on to say, "...for as yet you have not come to the rest and the inheritance which the LORD your God is giving you" (Deuteronomy 12:9).

So long as Christians are busy doing for God what is best in their own eyes, they will never enter into His rest and the true inheritance that is theirs to enjoy *now.* They will only be sweating it out, and end up weary, discouraged, depressed. They will likely become deeply cynical.

They will finally want to quit, and quit they must. They must quit depending on self-effort, and instead recognize the Truth: "I cannot—God never said I could; but *God can,* and always said He would!"

True repentance says, "I cannot," and true faith adds, "But God, You can!" Then you can reign in life as you let God be God, and you allow Him to show you that He is big enough for the job.

Reflect again on this truth: *Righteousness* is doing right in God's eyes, and God alone is the author of righteousness. For any activity of yours or mine to produce righteousness, God Himself must be the source of it. Are you allowing Him to do this in your life?

Our power and ability and sufficiency are from God.

2 CORINTHIANS 3:5, AMP

↠ In what particular aspect of your life at this time do you need to learn to say to God, "I cannot, but You can"?

↠ In what particular areas of life are you facing discouragement or cynicism?

↠ Are you allowing God to be the author of righteousness in your life?

What Kind of a Christian?

God is the absolute source of righteousness, but there is also an absolute source of unrighteousness—the devil. All human activity derives from one or the other of these two origins.

That is why the Bible says, "Whatsoever is not of faith is sin" (Romans 14:23, KJV). Whatever does not derive from your attitude of total dependence upon God, whatever does not release God's activity through your life, is sin. It is sin because it stems from an attitude of independence that makes you open to any and all of Satan's deceptions in his long history of usurping God's authority.

Every step you take, every attitude you adopt, every decision you make, everything you do and all you hope to be, is either in dependence upon the God who created you as His own dwelling place, or else the byproduct of the demon spirit of this world, "who now works in the sons of disobedience" (Ephesians 2:2), and who perpetuates his lies through a mindset of self-reliance in fallen humanity.

The Bible calls this attitude of independence a "carnal

mind" (Romans 8:7). It is a mind that is set "on the things of the flesh" rather than on "the things of the Spirit" (Romans 8:5). It means exercising the faculties of your personality in ways that are not dependent on the God whose presence alone imparts to you the quality of true humanity that He always intended for you.

It means thinking godlessly. In other words, thinking lightlessly, with a mind still in darkness. You take a step, you make a decision, you conceive your plans, you assume a responsibility, all without relating the situation to God and to His light and to all that He is within you.

This carnal mind can be in the believer just as much as in the unbeliever. Carnal or fleshly Christians have been regenerated by the restoration of the Holy Spirit to their human spirit, but in certain ways they still repudiate the Spirit's legitimate right to reestablish the rule of Christ in their minds, in their emotions, and in their wills. Although they profess Christ as Redeemer, their actions and decisions typically are taken for the sake of their own interests and for who they are in themselves, rather than for God's interests and for who He is. Their minds are still the plaything and the workshop of the devil, for the devil is smart enough and cunning enough that he can always persuade countless numbers of professing Christians to try and be Christians without Christ. They are willing to do anything for Jesus' sake, but they fail to understand that *His presence* is absolutely imperative to do it, that without Him we are nothing, have nothing, and can do nothing.

To be a carnal Christian is still to claim the right to exercise your own jurisdiction, make your own decisions and plans, choose your own pathway. But you will be useless to God, and you will make it into heaven only "as through fire" (1 Corinthians 3:15).

What kind of Christian do you want to be? To choose to be a carnal Christian is to choose spiritual oblivion. But if you decide genuinely that Christ must be everything and have everything in your life, if you say in your heart, "I want nothing less than to be all that for which the blood of God's dear Son was shed," then He is ready to lead you into discoveries that can completely revolutionize your whole humanity for time and eternity.

He who sins is of the devil.

1 JOHN 3:8

→ In what ways might there be some self-dependence behind any current plans or decisions that you may have made? Of what current attitudes or actions of self-dependence in your life do you need to repent?

→ In the responsibilities, duties, and activities that lie immediately ahead of you, what can you identify as God's purposes and interests? What is He wanting to accomplish?

→ What kind of Christian do you truly want to be? How would you express this in your own words?

The Shattered Interlock

God warned Adam: "In the day that you eat of it you shall surely die" (Genesis 2:17).

Did Adam die physically on the day when he fell to Satan's temptation and ate the fruit from the tree of the knowledge of good and evil? No, Adam did not die physically until he was more than nine hundred years of age. But when he defied and disobeyed God that day in the Garden of Eden, Adam did indeed die. What kind of death was it?

Death is the absence of life. What life did Adam lose that day? The Life of God! God withdrew His Holy Spirit from Adam's spirit. This was spiritual death.

As we have seen, God intended that a threefold moral interlock should govern our relationship to God and God's relationship to us:

1. Our *love* for God, reciprocating His love for us. This love is evidenced exclusively by…

2. Our *dependence* on God, because He created us in such a way that His presence is indispensable to our humanity and true function. This dependence can be expressed only by…

3. Our *obedience* to God.

This threefold moral interlock was shattered on that day in the Garden of Eden when man believed the devil's lie, the lie that man can somehow be man without God, that the Creator is not indispensable to the creature, that we can carve our own destiny, be king in our own kingdom, be our own god.

At this point of moral option, Adam fell, and at once things went wrong and have been going wrong ever since.

Picture in your mind a beehive (to take just one example in the amazing vastness of the animal kingdom) where tens of thousands of bees all operate by instinct in performing their particular jobs—the queen bee who lays eggs, plus the scout bees, the worker bees, the nurse bees, the guard bees, and others. They all carry out their individual tasks by God's design for the continuing health and propagation of the hive.

Now imagine that one day the rigid interlock between the instinctive thrust and each bee's soul suddenly snapped. All at once it was every bee for himself. What would happen?

The result, of course, would be anarchy, chaos, and self-destruction, which is precisely what has been evidenced in the history of mankind all down through the centuries. Through Satan's lying subtlety, mankind embarked upon the mad experiment of disobedience and human self-sufficiency, in which we are still today so heavily and tragically involved, with all its terrible consequences.

Without God, we are like an animal, only worse. God did not create man to be an animal, governed only by instinct. Our "natural" man, who we are in our "flesh," is void of true spirituality.

As heirs of a fallen Adam, we are born without any conscious sense either of a relationship with God or a capacity to have that relationship, even though this lack leaves instinctively a religious longing within us. Inherently we know there is a sort of vacuum inside which we try to fill with anything and everything apart from God Himself (Ephesians 4:17–18), with full cooperation from Satan.

It is amazing with what enthusiasm human beings are prepared to allow their humanity to be prostituted by the devil! Nevertheless, though they seek to justify themselves and be persuaded of the virtue of their actions, there is still an intangible restlessness within that leaves them baffled and perplexed.

Are there such moments of perplexity in your life—a restless soul whispering that all is not well with you?

You should no longer walk as the rest of the Gentiles walk, in the futility of their mind, having their understanding darkened, being alienated from the life of God, because of the ignorance that is in them, because of the blindness of their heart.

EPHESIANS 4:17-18

→   Have you experienced a restlessness of soul, a whispering within that all is not well with you? If so, what do you recognize as the reason for this, from God's viewpoint?

39

9

A Question of Parentage

Every act of sin has its origin in Satan; it is his character incarnate. "He who sins is of the devil, for the devil has sinned from the beginning" (1 John 3:8).

Likewise, every act of righteousness has its origin in God; it is *His* character incarnate.

In everything you do, the true character of a particular act can always be discerned in the authorship of that act. It is not a question of pattern, but of parentage.

That which is born of God in you is Jesus Christ, and it is He who does not commit sin, nor *can* He, for He is God! This is what the apostle John means when he writes, "Whoever has been born of God does not sin, for His seed remains in him; and he cannot sin, because he has been born of God" (1 John 3:9). The divine seed within us is the very nature of God Himself, and the nature that He wants to share with you through His Son.

Share the nature of Christ and you share His victory. You do not *achieve* it; you receive it, for Christ Himself "became for us wisdom from God—and righteousness and sanctification and redemption" (1 Corinthians 1:30).

To be dominated by the "flesh" is to be dominated by the devil; and to be dominated by the Holy Spirit is to be dominated by God.

What really is this "flesh" of which the Bible speaks? The flesh is that perverted principle in human beings which perpetuates Satan's proud hostility and enmity against God. In our fallen condition, every person's soul is dominated by the flesh and destitute of the Holy Spirit. You and I were born in this unregenerate condition.

The Holy Spirit and the flesh are inveterate foes: "For the flesh lusts against the Spirit, and the Spirit against the flesh; and these are contrary to one another, so that you do not do the things that you wish" (Galatians 5:17). That is why any steps God takes to reestablish His law in our hearts are resisted tooth and nail. Being already entrenched within the human soul by nature, the flesh is in a commanding position to incite the mind, the emotions, and the will of unregenerate persons (and of carnal Christians) to defy God and resist His grace.

The Holy Spirit always exposes the flesh for what it is, and there is nothing more infuriating to the carnally minded

Christian than when those who are spiritually discerning remain unimpressed with him in spite of so much self-advertisement.

The crucified, risen, and living Lord Jesus alone can put the noose around the neck of your flesh and keep your flesh where it belongs, and this He does by His Holy Spirit. You cannot carry out the execution, but to you and to you alone belongs the moral responsibility of confirming the sentence of death.

This is the decision God is waiting for you to make, for in His sovereignty God limits Himself by that simple law of faith which gives to you the moral capacity to know Him and to love Him for yourself.

Consent, therefore, to die to all that you are which does not derive from all that Christ is, and thank Him for His willingness to make it real in your experience.

> *To be carnally minded is death, but to be spiritually minded is life and peace.*
>
> ROMANS 8:6

+ What step of faith is God waiting for you to take in dying to your flesh?

+ Have you adequately expressed your thankfulness to God for the Holy Spirit's work in exposing the sinfulness of your flesh? Do this now.

10

The Ways of the Flesh

You may have harnessed the energy of the flesh in an otherwise quite genuine desire to honor the Lord Jesus in your life. The flesh, which has its origin in Satan, will go along with you; to survive, it is quite prepared to engage in every form of Christian activity, even though this may seem to honor Christ.

The flesh will sing in the choir, teach Sunday school, preside at a deacons' meeting, preach from the pulpit, organize an evangelistic crusade, go to Bible college, volunteer for the mission field, and a thousand other things, all of which may in themselves be otherwise legitimate, if only it can keep its neck out of the noose. The flesh will threaten, shout, strut, domineer, sulk, plot, creep, beg, plead, or sob, whatever the situation may demand in the interests of its own survival. By any and all means it will seek to cause every Christian to live by his own strength instead of by the power and grace of the Lord Jesus, and to conclude that doing so is actually a good thing!

The characteristic of the spiritually immature is that they are unable to discern between good and evil (Hebrews

5:13–14), and the baby Christian, like the foolish Galatians, "having begun in the Spirit" still tries to be "made perfect by the flesh" (Galatians 3:3).

We must be particularly patient with those whose lack of understanding allows a genuine love for the Lord Jesus to be satisfied with, and sometimes to be quite enthusiastic about, Christian activities involving means and methods which are heavily contaminated by the flesh. These are more deserving of instruction than rebuke, for they are still in their spiritual babyhood.

True spiritual conviction is an activity of the Holy Spirit within the human spirit, and when the Holy Spirit begins to convict you of your immaturity, bearing witness to your conscience that the Lord Jesus Christ is being denied His rightful place in your life, the old Adam-nature within you becomes irritable and edgy. At the same time it will seek to produce the most plausible arguments in justification of its own illegitimate activities, even though these activities are only what the Bible calls "dead works" (Hebrews 6:1; 9:14) and not the "good works" which are truly the work of God.

The Lord Jesus said, "This is *the work of God,* that you believe in Him whom He sent" (John 6:29). The work of God is your living faith in the adequacy of the One who is *in you,* which releases His divine action *through you.* This is the kind of activity that the Bible calls "good works" (Matthew 5:16, Ephesians 2:10), as opposed to "dead works."

"Good works" are those that have their origin in Jesus Christ, as Christ's activity is released through your body because you present it to Him as a living sacrifice. You do this only by a faith that expresses total dependence, as opposed to the Adamic independence (Romans 12:1–2).

God does not honor men and women and their deeds or their books or their organizations. The Father in heaven delights to honor *His Son*. It is only the Life of the Lord Jesus—His activity, *clothed* with you and *displayed* through you—that ultimately will find the approval of God.

Whatever you do [no matter what it is] in word or deed, do everything in the name of the Lord Jesus and in dependence upon His Person, giving praise to God the Father through Him.

COLOSSIANS 3:17, AMP

+ What "Christian activities" have you pursued more out of the energy of the flesh than in true dependence on the activity of Christ?

+ For any activity in your life, how can you go about assessing whether you are pursuing it in dependence on Christ instead of in the energy of the flesh?

+ In what ways does your flesh try to justify its own illegitimate activities in your life?

11

From Ignorance to Righteousness

There is a lie that Satan continues to propagate today with signal success in the hearts of countless people. It is the notion that by giving themselves back to the God who made them, and by submitting themselves to His sovereignty, they will be robbed of that liberty which makes life really worth living. Such people are not necessarily insincere in this conviction, but are the victims of their own ignorance, which makes them dupes of the devil, whose greatest delight is exploiting that ignorance.

God's Word describes in detail this ignorance and the devil's part in it:

> For the god of this world has blinded the unbelievers' minds [that they should not discern the truth], preventing them from seeing the illuminating light of the Gospel of the glory of Christ (the Messiah), Who is the Image and Likeness of God.
>
> 2 CORINTHIANS 4:4, AMP

Their moral understanding is darkened and their
reasoning is beclouded. [They are] alienated
(estranged, self-banished) from the life of God [with
no share in it; this is] because of the ignorance (the
want of knowledge and perception, the willful blindness) that is deep-seated in them, due to their
hardness of heart [to the insensitiveness of their
moral nature].

EPHESIANS 4:18, AMP

This hardened heart is the essence of the "old man"
within us (Ephesians 4:22), our flesh. The soul of the unregenerate is sold out to the flesh, and that person's behavior is
subject to the demands of a rebel regime that denies to God
His right to be God.

The human soul, dominated by the flesh, becomes party,
however unwittingly, to every carnal ambition that would
silence the voice of God and resist the claims of His Holy
Spirit.

The Lord Jesus Christ wants so very much to replace, by
His presence within you, all your inherent potential for evil
under the influence of the flesh. He offers you instead all His
limitless potential for good through the energy and power of
His indwelling Holy Spirit.

Spiritual new birth involves the principle of divine substitution, and though you are to be persuaded of your
inherent wickedness, you are to be equally persuaded of
Christ's inherent righteousness and all that it means for you.

If that which is born of the flesh is flesh, you can be

equally certain that that which is born of the Spirit is Spirit—
that God is God!

What is so completely amazing is that God is prepared to
be God in you not figuratively, but *factually.* You can actually
share His Life and be transformed into His likeness.

For His divine power has bestowed upon us
all things that [are requisite and suited] to
life and godliness, through the [full, personal]
knowledge of Him Who called us by and to
His own glory and excellence (virtue). By
means of these He has bestowed on us His
precious and exceedingly great promises, so
that through them you may escape [by flight]
from the moral decay (rottenness and
corruption) that is in the world because of
covetousness (lust and greed), and become
sharers (partakers) of the divine nature.

2 PETER 1:3–4, AMP

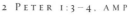

→ In what ways have you been tempted to think that by giving yourself to God, you would be missing out on certain freedoms and pleasures?

→ What does it mean practically to you that by your spiritual new birth, Christ's inherent righteousness is now yours?

→ At this time, how do you recognize that you are sharing the life of Christ in actuality?

12

What Really Is Sin?

in includes all the lies that the human race has been telling about God the Creator down through the centuries.

Sin is universal and represents the margin of difference between all that God is (in whose image we were made) and what we are on our own.

Sin is anything that falls short of God's glory (Romans 3:23), so that God will evaluate sin as any behavior that falls short of what *He* does, what *He* says, and what *He* is.

Sin therefore is exposed simply by relating our behavior to God's behavior. God is perfect, and by that perfection you and I can recognize sin, because sin is anything which falls short of His perfection.

God Himself is therefore the only standard by which sin is recognizable.

Sin also is defined in the Bible as faithless independence: "Whatever is not from faith is sin" (Romans 14:23). It is an attitude of "lawlessness" (1 John 3:4).

In light of this understanding of sin, what then does repentance involve?

Repentance means stepping out of independence back into dependence, and the measure of your repentance will be the measure of your dependence. Every area of your life in which you have not learned to be truly dependent on God is an area of your life in which you have not as yet repented.

Christ died for us so that He, risen and alive, might now come and dwell within us, so that we might no longer be egocentric, self-oriented, living only for our own interests: "He died for all, that those who live *should live no longer for themselves, but for Him* who died for them and rose again" (2 Corinthians 5:15).

Never be sorry for your *self.* Just be sorry for your sin!

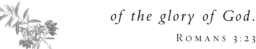

All have sinned and fall short

of the glory of God.

ROMANS 3:23

+ Is there any area of your life in which you have not learned to be truly dependent on God? If so, what repentance is necessary and appropriate at this time?

+ In your own behavior at this time, how are you falling short of all that God does, all that He says, and all that He is?

13

The Perfect Man

Since Adam fell, only one person has been normal. For thirty-three years, the Lord Jesus walked this earth to demonstrate normality, to demonstrate man as God created man to be. He was prepared to be man as God created man to be, constantly affirming the centrality of the Father.

After reminding us that God is invisible—"No one has seen God at any time"—John in his Gospel goes on to tell us this about Jesus: "The only begotten Son, who is in the bosom of the Father, He has declared Him." Or, as the *Amplified Bible* renders those last four words, "He has revealed Him and brought Him out where He can be seen; He has interpreted Him and He has made Him known" (John 1:18).

Although a man can never become God, God can choose to behave as a man at any time He so pleases. This is exactly what happened in the person of our Lord Jesus. Eternally, timelessly, He is never less than God, but He deliberately chose for those thirty-three years to behave fully as Man.

By being willing therefore to empty Himself and to humble Himself in being born as a human being (Philippians 2:6–8) clothed with *our* humanity, the Lord Jesus advertised Deity through everything He did, said, and was, allowing that Deity to be heard, seen, known, and loved.

This is why Jesus could tell Philip, "He who has seen Me has seen the Father…. The words that I speak to you I do not speak on My own authority; but the Father who dwells in Me does the works" (John 14:9–10). He was fulfilling the role for which God created you and me: to live and act in the image of God, fully displaying the truth about Him.

On the day of Pentecost, Peter described Christ in this way: "Jesus of Nazareth, *a Man* attested by God to you by miracles, wonders, and signs which God did through Him in your midst" (Acts 2:22). It was God Himself who did these miraculous works through Christ *the Man*. God was at work in and through the Lord Jesus, in the completeness, sinlessness, and perfection *of His humanity*. Here was man as God intended man to be! Here was true normality, as evidenced by the good works which God the Father accomplished through His Son and which He now wants to accomplish through you.

This is the divine vocation into which you have been redeemed: "For we are His workmanship, created *in Christ*

Jesus for good works, which God prepared beforehand that we should walk in them" (Ephesians 2:10). You are called and created in Christ Himself for a preordained life of good works.

This vocation can be fulfilled only in the energy and power of the One who indwells you now by His Spirit, just as He once walked only in the energy and power of the Father who indwelt Him through the Spirit. Of Himself He said, "The Son can do nothing of Himself" (John 5:19), and of you He says, "Without Me you can do nothing" (John 15:5).

Therefore expect and allow Christ to work in and through you just as Christ, in His life on earth, expected and allowed the Father to work in and through Him. Expect Him to do this…and He *will.* Just say "Thank You"—and let Him surprise you!

For as the Father has life in Himself, so He has granted the Son to have life in Himself.

JOHN 5:26

→ In your present understanding, what is your calling and vocation—the good works in this life which you were created to do in Christ Jesus?

→ How freely are you expecting and allowing Christ to work in and through you?

14

Out of Heaven and Into Us

You are driving down the highway in your car, and you see a fellow standing next to his car which is parked beside the road. Out of the kindness of your heart you stop and say, "Can I help?"

You discover that his car is out of gas. It does not have what it takes to keep going.

You happen to have a tow-rope in your trunk, so you offer to tow his car to the next town where he can fill up, and he agrees.

After you make it to the gas station and his car is filled with gas, the man tells you, with great embarrassment, that he just realized he has no money or even a credit card to pay for the gas. Again, out of the generosity of your heart, you pay the bill. You pay a debt you did not owe because *he* owes a debt he cannot pay.

What does that sound like? Redemption! That is what happened for us on the cross.

There is a purpose behind your payment of that man's

debt. What is it? To fill the tank and give the man what it takes for his car to go, so he can be on his way.

After you pay for the man's gas, he thanks you profusely, and you turn and walk away. As you get into your own car, you look back to wave good-bye. To your astonishment, you see the man straining behind his car, pushing it.

So you go back to him. What will you say? Probably something with words similar to these: "Poor, silly, thoughtless, unreflecting, senseless man!"—just the way Paul addressed the Galatians (Galatians 3:1, AMP) for failing to live simply by faith in the power of the indwelling Christ through His Spirit.

When you and I received Christ as our Redeemer, He gave us, through His Holy Spirit, the fullness and power of His resurrection. He has given us everything we could ever need at any time, under any circumstance. He gave us a car with a full tank; have you instead been trying to push it?

Whenever the gasoline is gone, it is not time for new upholstery, new spark plugs, or new tires; it is time to fill up the tank! Likewise if our spiritual tank is empty, it is time to fill it. With what? With *Christ*.

The Lord Jesus came from heaven to earth not just to get us out of hell and into heaven—though He is the only One who can and does, if we let Him—but to get Himself out of heaven and into us.

He gave Himself *for* us to give Himself *to* us, the gift of His Life, so that we may enjoy a wonderful, personal relationship with Him that never changes, because "Jesus Christ is the same yesterday, today, and forever" (Hebrews 13:8). Grasp this well, for otherwise your Christianity will remain boring, sterile, and impersonal. Christ Himself is the very life-content of the Christian faith. He is oil for the lamp and gas for the car. Only He makes everything "tick."

Christ did not die simply that you might be saved from a bad conscience, or even to remove the stain of past failure, but to "clear the decks" for His divine activity through you.

Christ is all and in all.

COLOSSIANS 3:11

✦ In what ways at this time is your relationship with Christ very wonderful and personal? Give Him thanks for this.

✦ In what ways is your Christianity in any way boring, or sterile, or impersonal?

15

What Is Eternal Life?

s eternal life simply a place you will go to after you are dead? Is it a peculiar feeling inside?

The apostle John tells us clearly what it is: "God has given us eternal life, and *this life is in His Son.* He who has the Son has life; he who does not have the Son of God does not have life" (1 John 5:11–12).

Jesus Christ and eternal life are synonymous terms; eternal life is none other than Jesus Christ Himself, of whom it is written, "In Him was life; and the life was the light of men" (John 1:4). If you have eternal life at all, it means that you have *Somebody;* you have the Son, Jesus Christ, just as He Himself affirmed: "I am the way, the truth, and the life" (John 14:6).

Eternal life is neither an inward feeling nor an ultimate destination after you are dead. If you are born again, eternal life is that quality of life that you possess right now, at this very moment, indwelling your physical body, with your own two feet on the ground, and in this world *today.* Where does this life come from? Only from Him. He *is* that Life. The life you possess is all of Him, and this is true salvation.

When I was a kid of twelve, a man told me about Jesus in a way I could understand. Then, unknown to him or anybody else, at a quarter till nine on a Saturday night, the thirteenth of August, 1927, I said in my heart, "Lord Jesus, nobody ever told me this before, that You died in my place. I gladly receive You so that You can forgive me." I knew He had become my Savior, and I have had that assurance ever since. I have never again had to receive the Lord Jesus Christ into my life because He did it then, according to His promise, and He always means what He says.

That moment and that event was *not* my salvation, however. My salvation, which I did not understand until about seven years later, is that Christ, having died for me to change my destination when I died, also rose again from the dead *to live His Life in me* and to change my character. His indwelling Life in me overcomes that old Adamic nature, the carnal mind that is at enmity with God and which can only abuse, misuse, and prostitute my humanity.

Salvation is so much more than a change of destination from hell to heaven! The true spiritual content of our gospel is not just heaven *one day*, but Christ *here and now*. In the economy of God, conversion is only an essential preliminary to discipleship, which is a lifetime of allowing Christ to live in you and do His work through you.

Your salvation is also a million times more than simply knowing your sins are forgiven. As a forgiven sinner you are to be reinhabited by your Maker, reinvaded by Deity, so that your humanity becomes intelligently available to an intelligent God for the intelligent purpose for which He intelligently created you. That is true sanctification, as the Bible explains it.

And this is eternal life: [it means] to know (to perceive, recognize, become acquainted with, and understand) You, the only true and real God, and [likewise] to know Him, Jesus [as the] Christ (the Anointed One, the Messiah), Whom You have sent.

JOHN 17:3, AMP

→ Do you have full and continual assurance of your salvation in Jesus Christ?

→ What does eternal life mean to you?

→ What does salvation mean to you?

16

The "Much More" of Your Salvation

f I asked you what the Lord Jesus has done to save you, almost instinctively you would say, "He *died* to save me."

That is the natural answer. Notice carefully, however, what Paul says in Romans 5:10. Through the death of Jesus we indeed "were reconciled to God"; and yet, "much more, having been reconciled, we *shall be saved* by His *life.*"

It is true that the death of Jesus saves us from the punitive consequence of sin and restores us to a true relationship with God after we were born spiritually dead, alienated from the life of God. Yet the very purpose of that new relationship is to enable us thereafter to *"be saved* by His *life,"* and this is the "much more" of our salvation.

Have you been reconciled to God by Christ's death? I hope you can say, "Yes, I can think back to the day when the Holy Spirit convicted me of the fact that I was a guilty sinner, and convinced me that the precious blood of Christ cleanses us from all sin. I remember the day when I deliberately received

Him as my personal Redeemer and put my trust in Him."

If you truly have been reconciled to God, then a perfectly logical question to ask would be, Are you *being* saved by Christ's life? The question is important because this is the "much more" of your salvation. If your Christian experience is limited only to being reconciled to God by the death of Christ, yet you are not *being* saved by the present reality of His Life, then you are obviously missing the "much more" of your salvation. In fact, you are missing the whole purpose for which Christ died. You are cheating Him of that for which His blood was shed.

Reconciled to God by Christ's death...and saved by His Life—the one is a crisis of the moment; the other is the process of a lifetime and on into eternity. The crisis precipitates the process. The crisis, if it is valid, should be followed by the process.

Reconciled to God by Christ's death, and being saved by His Life—the crisis involves an initial *act* of faith that accepts Christ for what He *did;* the process involves an *attitude* of faith that continues to enjoy all that Christ *is.* For He not only died for what you have *done;* He rose again from the dead to take the place of what you *are,* which He does by His Holy Spirit indwelling you.

This is the gospel, the whole of it. Anything less than this falls short of the gospel as revealed in the Word of God.

For if when we were enemies
we were reconciled to God
through the death of His Son,
much more, having been reconciled,
we shall be saved by His life.

Romans 5:10

→ What to you is the "much more" in your relationship with Christ? How do you understand this in your own mind?

→ From what has Christ saved you *today?* Respond to Him in thankfulness.

→ An attitude of true faith will enjoy Christ for who He is. What is it that you enjoy about Christ at this moment?

17

Your True Purpose

I wonder if you have noticed a seemingly strange statement which Jesus made in John 12:44: "Then Jesus cried out and said, 'He who believes in Me, believes not in Me but in Him who sent Me.'"

What Jesus meant was that to believe in Him was really to believe in the Father who sent Him.

In other words: "When you look at Me as Man, and listen to Me as Man (because of My normality and the absolute perfection of My humanity), you are seeing and listening to My Father. For everything I say is what My Father says. Everything I do is what He does. Everything I am is what He is, for as Man I have come to demonstrate to you perfect Manhood, the complete, unblemished expression of the divine Life of My Father."

So when you believe in Jesus as the Son of God, you are believing in God who indwells and fills the Man Jesus with Himself. This is normality, the image of Him who indwells and fills the real Man Jesus with Himself. That is why on this occasion Jesus went on to say, "He who sees Me sees Him who sent Me" (John 12:45). This was perfect manhood, humanity in perfection.

Now do not misunderstand me. There never was a moment of time in which the Lord Jesus as Man was not God. He is the eternal God, and was God in the beginning, with God His Father. But when He came into this world, He came to be *Man* as God always intended all mankind to be. Both for Jesus as well as for us, this perfect manhood, this perfect humanity, consists in the clear and complete manifestation of the Father.

That is why when Philip said, "Lord, show us the Father, and it is sufficient for us," Jesus replied in this way: "Have I been with you so long, and yet you have not known Me, Philip? He who has seen Me has seen the Father" (John 14:8–9). To see Jesus in His perfect humanity is to see God.

The Lord Jesus came into this world to redeem us and to restore us to our true humanity and function, to restore us to the Life that was lost in Adam, so that we can be in Him and He can be in us. Therefore the measure in which His redemptive purpose has been accomplished in us is the measure in which what *we* are is what *He* is, and what *we* do is what *He* does, and what *we* say is what *He* says. This is called *sanctification*, and it is the highest measure of Christ's regenerative work being accomplished in our lives.

In simple essence, the word *sanctification* refers to something that is being put to its correct use; it means the fulfillment of the purpose for which it was originally intended. As the Lord Jesus Christ walked on earth as Man,

He presented His body to the Father so that His humanity might be put to its intended purpose, and that purpose was to demonstrate and express the divine Life—to manifest God the Father.

The same is true for you and for me. What the Father was to Jesus in His humanity during His life on earth, so Jesus is to us in our humanity now. Just as Jesus' humanity was fully a manifestation of the Father's Deity, so our humanity now is to be a full expression of the Son's Deity. It is a relationship with Jesus that allows Him to live His Life through us, so that we do His work His way, when and where He may demand it.

When we as human beings make ourselves available to Jesus Christ in the same way that Jesus as Man made Himself available to the Father, then Jesus will be to us in our humanity what the Father was to Him in His humanity. That is the whole Christian life in a nutshell!

This is the sanctification which is God's will for you, so that your humanity can be used according to the purpose for which God created it.

For this is the will of God,

your sanctification.

1 THESSALONIANS 4:3

→ What is the "correct use" for which your own life is intended? What is God's will for you? How do you tend to understand this from your own perspective?

→ For the day and the moments that lie immediately ahead of you, do you have faith that the Lord Jesus will speak His words through your words, and live out His actions through your actions? With all your faith in Him, thank Him for what He will do.

→ In the days and moments ahead, how can you more fully make yourself available to Christ?

18

Seeing God in Action

One day as He was walking along, Jesus "saw a man who was blind from birth." His disciples also saw the man, and immediately they asked Jesus one of their typically stupid questions (I am always encouraged when I see the disciples doing that): "Rabbi, who sinned, this man or his parents, that he was born blind?" (John 9:1–2).

Jesus answered, "Neither this man nor his parents sinned" (John 9:3). Jesus of course was not saying that the blind man and his parents were not sinners. Jesus knew perfectly well that "there is none righteous, no, not one" (Romans 3:10). Jesus instead was saying that this man's physical disability was not in any way the direct result of a particular sinful action either on his part or on that of his parents. Of course there is such a thing as a permanently damaging effect in a person's life that is brought about by his own wrong and stupid actions (do not blame God for that), but the idea that every physical disability derives from some particular act of sin is nonsense.

Jesus went on to give the truly important reason for this man's blindness: "that *the works of God* should be revealed in him" (John 9:3). Jesus was saying, "This man is blind so that you can see *how God goes about His business.* You are going to see God at work; you are going to see *God in action.*"

Considering that the Lord Jesus has promised to send *us* in the same way the Father sent Him (John 20:21), you and I ought to learn something from this story. This incident shows us how the Lord Jesus, as God, will go about His business in *us,* revealing the works of God.

How should we define "the works of God"? Quite obviously, the work of God is God Himself at work. If it is not God Himself doing the work, it is not a work of God.

This is exactly what Jesus allowed the world to see in His own life on earth. Through the record of that life in the Scriptures, He is telling us this: "As I live through My Father and the world sees My Father at work in Me, so also those who will appropriate Me, those who enter into a living and vital faith relationship with Me, will allow the world to see Me at work in them."

Therefore, in watching Jesus interact with the blind man in John 9, we will see God in action.

What do we see first?

"When He had said these things, He spat on the ground" (John 9:6). Here we are with the disciples waiting and watching to see God in action, and Jesus *spits*. The Lord Jesus has a marvelous sense of humor!

From His spit on the ground, Jesus then made clay, anointed the blind man's eyes with it, and told him to go and wash it off. "So he went and washed, and came back seeing" (9:7).

Who healed the blind man?

God did! This was one of the "miracles, wonders, and signs which *God did* through Him" (Acts 2:22). In the totality of His humanity, the Lord Jesus was available to the Father; He was "being filled with the Holy Spirit" (Luke 4:1), just as we are commanded always to be (Ephesians 5:18).

Jesus said, "I always do those things that please Him" (John 8:29). He was telling us, "If My Father wants to preach through My lips, I am available for Him to do so. If My Father wants to raise a man from the dead, I will give the commanding word. If My Father wants to walk on water, My feet are at His disposal. Oh, and by the way, if My Father wants to spit, I spit!" Jesus was simply being a Man in true normality, inhabited by His Father. He had given His Father total right of way to do as He pleased in His life. How marvelous!

When was the Lord Jesus being filled the most with the Holy Spirit? It was at *all* times, whether preaching or spitting. He was available to the Father day and night—preach or spit.

Are *you* that available to Christ?

> *God anointed Jesus of Nazareth with the*
>
> *Holy Spirit and with power.*
>
> ACTS 10:38

→ Have you presented your body to the Lord who indwells you, so that He may do His works in your body? Do this in a new and fresh way today.

19

Real Spirituality

t is not the *nature* of what you do that determines the spirituality of any action, but the *origin* of what you do. There was never a moment in the life of the Lord Jesus that was without divine significance, because there was never anything He did, never anything He said, never any step He took which did not spring from a divine origin. There was nothing in His life that was not the activity of the Father in and through the Son. He lived out thirty-three years of availability to the Father, so that the Father in and through Him might implement the program that had been established and agreed upon between the Father and the Son before the world was even created.

Why did the Father give all things into the Son's hands? Because Jesus Christ was completely *Man,* and He was completely Man because He was completely *available.* For the first time since Adam fell into sin, there was on earth a man as God intended man to be.

Which of His activities was the more "spiritual": preaching the Sermon on the Mount, raising Lazarus from the dead, or washing His disciples' feet? The answer, of course, is that no one activity was more spiritual than another, for all had their origin in the Father, who acted through the Son. That is why Jesus could say, "I always do those things that please Him" (John 8:29).

The Lord Jesus summarized this in John 14:10: "Do you not believe that I am in the Father, and the Father in Me? The words that I speak to you I do not speak on My own authority; but *the Father who dwells in Me does the works.*" In other words, "I have presented My body to the Father who indwells Me, that He may do His works in My body. My Father does His works through His Spirit indwelling Me, and through His Spirit I have offered Myself without fault to My Father."

The whole activity of the Lord Jesus on earth as Man was the Father's activity in the Son, through the eternal Spirit, as Jesus presented His body to the Father through the Spirit. This is true also for us. Our spirituality is simply our availability to God for His divine activity, and the *form* of this activity is irrelevant.

If it pleases you, always and only, to do what pleases God…you can do as you please!

> *Jesus of Nazareth…went about doing*
> *good…for God was with Him.*
> ACTS 10:38

✤ How eager are you to do whatever pleases God?

20

Letting the Father
Handle the Situation

he Lord Jesus acted at all times on the assumption that His Father was handling the situation, and Jesus simply took care to obey His Father's instructions. Even when He was being reviled and tortured, "He left his case in the hands of God" (1 Peter 2:23, NLT).

By this submission to His Father, Jesus "learned obedience" (Hebrews 5:8) as a Man, and the obedience was total: "He humbled Himself and became obedient *to the point of death,* even the death of the cross" (Philippians 2:8).

Now, as God, He asks the same of you and me.

This is what baffled the disciples. At times they must have thought the Lord Jesus was hopelessly passive, and that He was failing to come to grips with reality. He seemed bent on drifting toward disaster. They must have wondered, *Why not get organized?* Why not cash in on His popularity with the crowd or pull some political strings? After all, money speaks, and for getting a movement off the ground, surely that rich young ruler could have exercised a positive influence before, unfortunately, he "went away sorrowful" after Jesus told him to sell his possessions and "come, take up the cross, and follow Me" (Mark 10:21–22).

Whenever Jesus performed some notable miracle and someone was healed, why did He avoid such obvious opportunities for wider publicity and tell people to keep their mouths shut? Why did He not throw His weight around, project His personality, exploit His authority, and confound His foes once and for all by some overwhelming vindication of His Deity? Why did He not emphatically let people know just who He was and where He had come from? Why did He not boldly justify His claim to equality with the Father and wipe the floor with His enemies? Why this pitiable show of weakness and this apparent foolishness?

Why? "Because the foolishness of God is wiser than men, and the weakness of God is stronger than men" (1 Corinthians 1:25). Therefore, "He was crucified in weakness" (2 Corinthians 13:4).

The Lord Jesus Christ could afford to be weak; He could afford to be thought foolish in the eyes of silly, sinful men; He could afford to be reviled and mocked and spat upon, because He knew He had been sent by the Father, and that into the Father's hands He had committed His Spirit, not only in death but throughout His life. Jesus could afford to do as He was told, and He could afford to die, because He knew that Someone else was taking care of the consequences: "For though He was crucified in weakness, yet *He lives by the power of God*" (2 Corinthians 13:4).

The resurrected Christ now *lives*, to continue His Life in you.

If you are not yet prepared to do as you are told, no matter how weak or foolish it will make you look, then whatever you believe about the resurrection of the Lord Jesus Christ is still academic. You have not yet entered into the good of it.

When it comes to the point of obedience to God's clear instructions, the Life of Jesus Christ within you makes human circumstances irrelevant; for to share His Life now as He once shared His Father's Life on earth is to know, as Jesus did, that Someone else is taking care of the consequences.

I do not mean by this that God's purposes are always irrational in the light of human circumstance, nor that there is any particular virtue in being eccentric or foolhardy. What I am urging is simply that you become delightfully detached from the pressure of circumstance, so that it ceases to be the criterion in the decisions you make. You do as you are told, whether God's instructions appear to be compatible with the immediate situation or not, and you leave God to vindicate Himself and to justify the course of action upon which you have embarked at His command.

You will not need to know what He plans to do with you…you simply need to know *Him*.

When I am weak, then I am strong.

2 CORINTHIANS 12:10

→ Are you fully prepared to do whatever God tells you to do?

→ In preparing to do God's will, do you find that you are delightfully detached from the pressure of circumstance, so that this pressure has ceased to be the criterion in the decisions you make?

→ Why can you afford to appear "weak" or "foolish" in the eyes of others as you obey the Lord's will?

21

Exceptional and Extraordinary

magine the scene somewhat like this:
First the sound of knuckles rapping on the door. *Knock-knock-knock-knock.*

"Come in."

A man opens the door and takes one step inside, then nods and says, "Thank you. Up so late?"

"Well, yes," the Lord Jesus replies. "I was waiting for you."

"What do you mean? How could you know I was coming, in the middle of the night?"

"You are no stranger to Me," Jesus answers, "though I am a stranger to you. Come in, Nicodemus, and sit down."

The Gospel of John tells us that Nicodemus came by night to Jesus and spoke these words: "Rabbi, we know that You are a teacher come from God; for no one can do these signs that You do unless God is with him" (John 3:2). He was saying, "Master, You are exceptional. You are extraordinary. I have come to the conclusion that *God* is the only possible explanation for what You do and what You say."

In response, I imagine the Lord Jesus saying, "You are absolutely right, Nicodemus. There is no possible explanation for what I do and say except God. But please do not misunderstand me, Nicodemus. This is true not because I am God, though God I am, but because I have chosen to live as Man in the way God created man to be. I place all of My humanity at My Father's disposal. I am available to Him in body, spirit, and soul—mind, emotions, and will.

"You are right, Nicodemus, I am exceptional. As a matter of fact, I am *the* exception.

"You are right that I am also extraordinary, but let Me tell you something: No matter how ordinary a person may be, put God in that person, and the ordinary becomes extraordinary."

All of this would make for astonishing news to Nicodemus. This man who came to Jesus by night was sincere and deeply religious, but he was also a fallen human being, and Jesus therefore let him know that religion could not save him: "I assure you, most solemnly I tell you, that unless a person is born again (anew, from above), he cannot ever see (know, be acquainted with, and experience) the kingdom of God" (John 3:3, AMP).

Though Nicodemus was a leader among the Pharisees, in his pathetic ignorance he had a big problem, one that is shared by many today who hold high positions in churches. He did not truly understand why and how God designed man to function, nor what had gone wrong. Instead Nicodemus was religiously house-trained to conform to certain religious patterns of thinking and acting. He had pious language…but no Life; ritual…but no reality. He had only sterile religion, a sad substitute for the real thing.

The *real* thing, as Jesus told Nicodemus, is "that which is born of the Spirit" (John 3:6). The Holy Spirit restores and connects us to the real thing, to the reality of humanity as God intended.

The simplest possible explanation and definition of the person of the Holy Spirit is this: Through the Holy Spirit, man can make himself available to God, and through the Holy Spirit, God is prepared to make Himself available to man. The Spirit becomes the agent of a mutual interavailability: All there is of God is available to every human being who is available to all there is of God, and the Holy Spirit brings this into our reality.

The faith through which we claim redemption through the blood of Christ is the very faith through which we receive the Holy Spirit, and we may not obtain one without the other. When through faith you claim redemption and the forgiveness of your sins through the blood of Christ shed vicariously for you, God is able to send His Holy Spirit into your human spirit.

Our bodies are designed as temples of the living God, and the special work of the Holy Spirit in your life and mine is to fill these bodies afresh with His glory, and cleanse them for His use as instruments of righteousness.

Ever be filled and stimulated with the Holy Spirit...at all times and for everything giving thanks in the name of our Lord Jesus Christ to God the Father.

EPHESIANS 5:18–20, AMP

→ Take time to thank the living God for the special work of His Holy Spirit in filling your body afresh with His glory, and cleansing your body for His use as an instrument of righteousness.

22

All of Truth

Truth is timeless. Truth was true then and is true now and will be true forever, because Truth is not a dogma or a creed. Truth is a Person.

The Lord Jesus said, "I am…the truth" (John 14:6).

Truth is not just a theology, the study of God, but a theocracy—being ruled by God. This means that for you and me there are no decisions to make, but only instructions to obey.

Jesus Christ Himself is the final exegesis of all truth. He is all that we need to know about God, and He is all that we need to know about man.

Being the truth about man, He demonstrates to us (by the way He lived then in His relationship to the Father) exactly how we are to live now in our relationship with Christ if we have opted out of Adam and into Christ to be restored to function by allowing Him to live through us. That is why we must keep our gaze constantly upon the person of the Lord Jesus Himself.

He was in the beginning with God, and was God, and is God, and as the Creative Word, all things were made by Him.

When He came to this earth, however, He became Man in the very fullest sense of the term, Man as God intended man to be. He behaved as God intended man to behave, walking day by day in that relationship to the Father which God had always intended should exist between man and Himself.

"I am the way, the truth, and the life" (John 14:6). When Jesus said, "I am the way," He was telling us, *"I* am how you can *become* a Christian, for I died for you." When He said, "I am the life," He was telling us, *"I* am how you can *be* the Christian you have become." Jesus is the Truth about the Way and the Truth about the Life.

In all His activities, in all His reactions, in every step He took, in every word He spoke, in every decision He made, He did so as Man, even though He was God. He knew that in His perfection as Man, He had been vested by the Father with all that God had originally intended to vest in man, which is "all things" (John 16:15, Romans 8:32; 1 Corinthians 3:21). In other words, a functional man has an unlimited call upon the inexhaustible supplies of Deity.

Jesus Christ was Perfect Man, totally, unrelentingly, unquestioningly available, and that is why "all things" were available to Him: "All things that the Father has are Mine" (John 16:15).

This is the Christ, the wonderful Savior whom Paul was so utterly determined to know when he said, "For my determined purpose is that I may know Him—that I may progressively become more deeply and intimately acquainted with Him, perceiving and recognizing and understanding the wonders of His Person more strongly and more clearly, and that I may in that same way come to know the power out-flowing from His resurrection" (Philippians 3:10, AMP). Paul's supreme ambition was not to learn new ministry techniques and methodologies or more insightful psychological solutions to human problems, but to *know Jesus Christ* and the illimitable power flowing from His resurrection.

Paul also kept in focus the promised result of this intimate acquaintance with Christ and His indwelling resurrection Life: "That if possible I may attain to the spiritual and moral resurrection that lifts me out from among the dead, even while in the body" (Philippians 3:11, AMP). By dwelling within us, the risen Lord, our Creator-Redeemer, lifts us out from among the dead even while we are still in the body, because we share His Life.

God wants all of us to know what Paul longed to know. He wants us to "know and understand what is the immeasurable and unlimited and surpassing greatness of His power in and for us who believe, as demonstrated in the working of His mighty strength, which He exerted in Christ when He raised Him from the dead and seated Him at His own right hand in the heavenly places" (Ephesians 1:19–20, AMP).

Grace and truth came through Jesus Christ.

JOHN 1:17

→ How have you found God's mighty strength within you to be "immeasurable and unlimited," as Paul did?

→ Are you utterly determined to *know* Christ as Paul did—that you may "progressively become more deeply and intimately acquainted with Him"?

23

God's DNA

The Lord Jesus, as the true Son of God, was miraculously conceived in the womb of His mother Mary by the Holy Spirit, and He was born complete with the Father's DNA—the Divine Nature from Above. "For in Him the whole fullness of Deity (the Godhead) continues to dwell in bodily form, giving complete expression of the divine nature" (Colossians 2:9, AMP).

The true believer in Christ now shares that same DNA, that same completeness: "You are in Him, made full and having come to fullness of life; in Christ you too are filled with the Godhead—Father, Son and Holy Spirit—and reach full spiritual stature" (Colossians 2:10, AMP).

What a birthright is ours in Christ! Through God's "precious and exceedingly great promises," not only do we "escape by flight from the moral decay (rottenness and corruption) that is in the world" but we also "become *sharers (partakers) of the divine nature*" (2 Peter 1:4, AMP).

It was God's original intention that by the indwelling of the Spirit of Christ, every human being should fully experience His Life and become a participant in the divine nature.

When this is established spiritually within your soul, it means that not only does the Lord Jesus Christ live by His Holy Spirit within your human spirit, but He now controls your mind, your emotions, and your will. By all that you do and say and are, His Life and likeness are expressed through you. People around you become aware of the fact, though they may not understand it, that by something God Himself has done, you have become a partaker of all that He is.

In Christ you too are filled with the Godhead—Father, Son and Holy Spirit—and reach full spiritual stature.... You were also raised with Him to a new life through your faith in the working of God as displayed when He raised Him up from the dead.

COLOSSIANS 2:10–12, AMP

→ How fully are you letting the Lord Jesus Christ control your mind and emotions and will through His Holy Spirit?

→ Are people around you becoming aware of your participation in the divine nature?

24

That Look of Confidence

There is something frighteningly authoritative about the look of quiet, unflinching confidence upon the face of someone who knows that he is right and at peace with God.

The face of Stephen, the first martyr, conveyed this look when the rulers in Jerusalem falsely brought him to trial: "All who sat in the council, looking steadfastly at him, saw his face as the face of an angel" (Acts 6:15). Stephen denounced their guilt without any suggestion of apology, without any hint of fear: "You stiff-necked and uncircumcised in heart and ears!

You always resist the Holy Spirit; as your fathers did, so do you" (Acts 7:51) Hearing these things, "they were cut to the heart" (Acts 7:54).

It was this look upon the face of the Lord Jesus Christ which, perhaps more than anything else, frightened Herod and Pontius Pilate on that day when Jesus stood trial before them, and they yielded to false accusations and to the cries of the crowd to crucify Him. A bad conscience is always uneasy in the presence of truth. You may shoot truth between the eyes when it looks you quietly in the face, but it will not be truth which falls victim to your bullet. It was not truth that lay bleeding and dying on the day Stephen was stoned to death; nor was it truth that hung upon a cross to be buried in a tomb, where sin was condemned and Satan himself judged and defeated.

That is why you can now be at peace with God, enjoying a peace that gives you that sense of quiet, unflinching confidence, a confidence that comes only from God, through Your trust in Him.

Paul could say, "Such is the reliance and confidence that we have *through Christ* toward and with reference to God" (2 Corinthians 3:4, AMP). It was an enduring confidence, despite Paul's many tribulations.

Perhaps you can personally identify with what Paul meant when he said, "We were so utterly and unbearably weighed down and crushed that we despaired even of life itself." If so, have you gone on, as Paul did, to know God as the One who is overwhelmingly adequate in the most hopeless situation? "Indeed," Paul went on to say, "we felt within ourselves that we had received the very sentence of death, but that was *to keep us from trusting in and depending on ourselves* instead of on God Who raises the dead. For it is He Who rescued and saved us" (2 Corinthians 1:9–10, AMP).

Paul was relying on *all that God is*, for God can actually raise the dead. Paul knew this truth: All that God is…is available to whoever is himself available to all that God is.

God…has given us the Spirit as a guarantee.

So we are always confident.

2 CORINTHIANS 5:5–6

→ How substantial is your level of peace and confidence these days?

→ When you have faced what seemed to be a hopeless situation, have you learned how God is overwhelmingly adequate?

25

Moving Beyond the Necessary Silence

There were times when Jesus found it necessary to silence His disciples to keep them from telling others about Him—because they did not know enough to talk sense.

Even on the occasion when Simon Peter confessed, "You are the Christ, the Son of the living God" (Matthew 16:16), we read this: "Then He commanded His disciples that they should *tell no one* that He was Jesus the Christ" (Matthew 16:20). Later, as Jesus and three of His disciples came down from the mountain where they had seen Jesus transfigured in glory, He again told them, *"Tell the vision to no one* until the Son of Man is risen from the dead" (Matthew 17:9).

Unless you know Jesus as the risen, living, and indwelling Savior, as a present-tense reality in your own heart and life, then Jesus wants you to keep your mouth shut, because you will not know enough about Him worth saying.

God *wants* you to know this reality that is worth talking about, to know Him in a new and a thrilling way for yourself. Life will then have become the adventure God intended it to be. Dead to yourself and alive to God, you will share the Life of Jesus Christ and you will share His victory, though a thousand temptations beset you.

You will also share Christ's compassion for the lost and become expendable for God in the service of mankind. The consuming passion of your soul will be to know Christ more fully and to make Him known.

You will remember how the hour came when, in the sinlessness of Christ's humanity in which He demonstrated the innocence of the pre-fallen Adam, there was laid upon Him the guilt of a whole race of fallen men: "I am going to die, Father, *for them,* so that without doing violence to the righteousness of a holy God, We can restore to mankind the Life that was lost in the day Adam fell—the Life of God. We can switch them on and make them functional."

When the Lord Jesus died for you, He not only paid the price of your redemption, but your Adam-nature was identified with Him and nailed to His cross—that old sinful nature which for so long has dominated your soul and frustrated all your hopes. This is something God wants you *to know:* "We *know* that our old (unrenewed) self was nailed to the cross with Him in order that our body, which is the instrument of sin, might be made ineffective and inactive for evil, that *we might no longer be the slaves of sin"* (Romans 6:6, AMP).

He bore our sins in His own body on the tree. He suffered, the just for the unjust. Then He rose again from the dead, because His reason for dying was to allow us to share His resurrection. Christ gave Himself *for* us to give Himself *to* us. His presence puts God back into the man. He came that we might have Life—God's Life.

In the years leading up to His death, the life Jesus lived was sinless, complete, perfect, and beautiful. Was that then all Jesus came to do—simply to give us a beautiful example to emulate? Was He saying, "Keep your eyes on Me and do your best to follow along"?

No. That would have been a message of futility. It could bring us nothing but despair.

It is not a matter of our doing our best for Him, but of *Christ being His best in us.* All that He is in all that we are! We can never have more…and need never enjoy less. Just receive and say, "Thank You!"

This is the good news that is ours to tell.

The life was manifested, and we have seen,
and bear witness, and declare to you that
eternal life which was with the Father and
was manifested to us.

1 JOHN 1:2

→ Have you known enough of the living and indwelling presence of the risen Jesus to be able to speak up about it?

→ Is knowing Christ and making Him known the consuming passion of your life?

26

The God-Given Life

There is a wonderful discovery God wants you to make, one that is absolutely basic to an intelligent understanding of the Christian life.

This discovery is not only charged with comfort and encouragement for your soul, but is calculated to deliver you from the heartbreak, frustration, and despair which are the unhappy lot of so many sincere Christians in their earnest endeavors to please God in the energy of the flesh.

It is not a question of improving or being reformed, but of substitution, receiving a God-given Life, a life for which we have nothing to offer to God in exchange.

God tells us that the old Adamic nature within you, called the flesh, has no redeeming feature about it. It is entirely without remedy.

This was Paul's persuasion: "For I know that nothing good dwells within me, that is, in my flesh. I can will what is right, but I cannot perform it. I have the intention and urge to do what is right, but no power to carry it out" (Romans 7:18, AMP).

For your own spiritual well-being, it is absolutely imperative that you recognize the fact that this old nature will never change its character. All the wickedness of which it is capable today, it will be capable of tomorrow, or fifty years from now if you are still alive. The flesh within you then will be as wicked as the flesh within you today, and there is absolutely no salvageable content within it.

What a relief it must be for you to discover that in all your attempts to harness the flesh in the service of Jesus Christ, and in all your painful endeavors to introduce it to godly principles of life and conduct, God has never expected anything of you but the hopeless failure you have been!

You have been trying to do the impossible!

The Galatian Christians had made the same mistake, for they had been trying to achieve holiness in their own strength. They tried to submit themselves to rules and regulations imposed upon them by legalists who gloried in their conformity to Jewish customs. Outward form and ritualistic patterns had become a substitute for the spontaneous expression of the indwelling Life of Christ.

Paul therefore addressed them as "poor and silly and thoughtless and unreflecting and senseless Galatians!" He asked them, "Did you receive the Holy Spirit as the result of obeying the Law and doing its works, or was it by hearing the message of the Gospel and believing it? Was it from observing a law of rituals or from a message of faith? Are you so foolish and so senseless and so silly? Having begun your new life spiritually with the Holy Spirit, are you now reaching perfection by dependence on the flesh?" (Galatians 3:1–3, AMP).

The flesh within you has never ceased to love sin, and never will. Given half a chance, it will always manifest its corruption and depravity.

This is why the godliest of men still have latent within them the most terrible potential for evil. It is the godliest of men who know it best, for it is the acknowledgment of this very fact which is the secret of their godliness. They have learned, often by bitter experience, that character does not change for the better by improving the flesh, but only by allowing it to be replaced by the Holy Spirit. Only the Holy Spirit can render its pernicious appetites inoperative.

"The heart is deceitful above all things, and desperately wicked" (Jeremiah 17:9). Be persuaded therefore of the wickedness of your own heart, and humbly confess it before God. Never be shocked or dismayed at the amazing capacity for sin that lies within you, for this is the nature of your case.

It is only when you are honest enough to face up to these facts that you will have, on the one hand, a big enough view of what the Lord Jesus Christ came into the world to do for you; and on the other hand, the desire to let Him do it!

Christ...is our life.

COLOSSIANS 3:4

→ In what ways have you been trying to do the impossible by attempting to harness the energy of the flesh in the service of Christ?

→ Have you fully recognized the fact that your flesh will never be improved or reformed, and will never cease to love sin?

→ Do you know the truth that you still have latent within you the most terrible potential for evil? If so, confess this before God in renewed appreciation for His gift to you of righteousness in Jesus Christ.

27

The End Product of True Evangelism

The end product of evangelism is not just to get you out of hell and into heaven, but to get God out of heaven and into you, so that Christ living in your heart might bring God out again into the open where He can be seen. That is what brings *glory* to God.

This happens when we are prepared to identify ourselves with Christ in His death and to share His resurrection Life: You acknowledge as a redeemed sinner that Jesus, risen from the dead, has come to reinvade your humanity so that you can place all that you are at His disposal. Others who look at you will see *Him* behaving, just as people looked at Jesus and saw the Father behaving.

This is the gospel.

What then is the ultimate end product of our obeying this gospel and entering into the good of that which has been provided for us in Christ to restore us to our true function as human beings?

God has predestined us "to be conformed to the image of His Son" (Romans 8:29). Therefore, when you are finally evangelized and people look at you, they should see the image of the Lord Jesus Christ. This is what God has always had in mind for us, from the eternal ages of the past.

That is why *Jesus* is the end product of evangelism—His Life indwelling you is exactly what God had in mind when He sent His Son to redeem you and to reconcile you to a holy God. He sent us His Son not just to get you and me out of hell and into heaven, but to get the God of heaven into you and me, so that Christ living in our hearts might be our hope of bringing God again out into the open where He can be seen, to His glory!

We identify ourselves with Him, saying as Paul did in Galatians 2:20, "I have been crucified with Christ," and we share His resurrection, just as Paul went on to explain in the same verse, "It is no longer I who live, but Christ lives in me"—not I, but Christ. Paul is saying, "I am a redeemed sinner, and the risen Jesus has come to reinvade my humanity so that He can serve with my hands, walk with my feet, speak with my lips, see with my eyes, hear with my ears, think with my mind, and love with my heart, so that to me, to live now is Christ. It is my privilege as a forgiven sinner to place my humanity at His disposal so that others looking at me will see *Him* behaving, just as those who looked at Jesus saw His Father behaving."

This is the gospel as we need to understand it, because the Lord Jesus said, "As the Father has sent Me, I also send you" (John 20:21)—sending us on the same terms and for the same purpose.

He is the Sender, and we are the sent ones, and for this reason the only authority you and I can legitimately exercise in any area of life is the authority that derives from our submission to His authority.

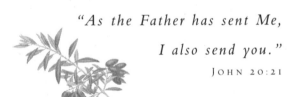

"As the Father has sent Me,
I also send you."
JOHN 20:21

→ How are you allowing the Lord Jesus to serve with your hands?

→ How can you allow Him to walk with your feet?

→ How can you allow Him to speak with your lips?

→ How can you allow Him to see with your eyes?

→ How can you allow Him to hear with your ears?

→ How can you allow Him to think with your mind?

→ How can you allow Him to love with your heart?

28

How He Gives Us Rest

Suppose you were digging a hole, and I offered to give you a rest. How would I do it?

While you continued shoveling, I could call down a suggestion to you, such as, "Try tossing the dirt over your left shoulder instead of your right." I could sing a song about digging, or discuss all the latest philosophical thinking that might relate to it.

Would any of that give you rest? No, it would more likely give you a heart attack!

Yet those approaches are very much like what today's Christianity tries to do to bring rest to struggling believers, all in vain.

How could I truly give you rest if you were in that hole digging? Obviously, there is only one way: You must get out and let me get in. You must drop the spade and let me pick it up. You must quit and let me take over. You must vacate that hole in the ground so that I can occupy it.

That is the way the Lord Jesus wants to give you and me rest. "Come to Me," He says, "all you who labor and are heavy laden, and *I will give you rest*" (Matthew 11:28). This is His offer. He is saying to us, "Get out, and let Me get in. Vacate, and let Me occupy. Drop the spade, and let Me dig!"

This is what happens when you take Christ at His word, when you come to Him and say, "Lord Jesus, I want the kind of rest that only You can give me." You bow yourself out and bow Him in. In true repentance you say, "Lord Jesus, I cannot, and You never said I could. You never expected me to do this on my own. All You have expected of me, apart from You sharing Your Life with me, is the failure that I have been on my own.

"It is true: I cannot—but in genuine confidence I acknowledge that You can! Therefore I will translate what I know and believe into faith, and I will let *You* do it. I will get out of this hole and let You get in. I vacate, so that You can occupy. I drop the spade so that You can pick it up."

Knowing this, and doing it, is such a relief!

What happens next? As you vacate, incredibly enough

the Lord *does* occupy. He surprises you beyond your wildest dreams. You discover at last that God is big enough for the job. Your heart is filled with joy, and this experience of His adequacy undergirds your faith for the next situation that arises when you recognize your need for Him, your need for His rest and for relief from your own ineffective self-effort.

Then when the next time of testing comes and you begin to feel weary and burdened once again, you can say, "Lord Jesus, thanks for what You did last time. It was fantastic. I had been baffled and could not see any possible solution to the problem I faced, but You came through magnificently. However, the situation I am facing now is ten times worse, but that is exciting, Lord Jesus, because this gives You ten times more opportunity to demonstrate that, as God, You are never less than big enough! So I thank You, for I am vacating and You are occupying."

To your amazement, magnificently He handles the situation in His own way and in His own time. You have learned to walk by faith, and every new experience of His adequacy undergirds your confidence as you receive more and more of His grace.

That is how we learn to grow in grace.

"Take My yoke upon you and learn from Me,
for I am gentle and lowly in heart, and you
will find rest for your souls."
MATTHEW 11:29

→ In what areas of effort do you need to let Christ take over?

→ How have you discovered that the Lord is big enough for the job of running your life when you trust Him by faith?

→ What growth do you see in your confidence and in your faith in Christ?

29

True Rest

Christian rest is *not* inactivity. Christian rest is rest because *He* carries the load.

Some people imagine that if you bow yourself out and bow the Lord Jesus in, if you die to self-effort and let God do it, that is passivity. Well, it is passivity only if you consider God to be passive, and only if you consider the Lord Jesus to be a weakling and incapable of running His own kingdom as King, and that of course is blasphemous.

If I think that by stepping aside and letting God handle it, *nothing* is going to happen, this only indicates that I do not really believe in God or in the competence of Jesus Christ. I am assuming that if it were not for folks like me doing the work and keeping God in business, He would be in bad shape. That is the only logical conclusion we can draw when anyone assumes, "If I let Jesus do it, nothing will happen."

When you are truly relaxed in the Lord and experiencing His true rest, that rest will nearly always involve *more* activity than we would otherwise ever know. That is because Christ is in action, and you in your humanity are simply the clothes of His divine activity.

This is the rest of faith. You relax, almost like a spectator, except that it is your hands with which He is at work, your lips with which He is speaking, your eyes with which He sees the need, your ears with which He hears the cry, and your heart with which He loves the lost.

To "let go and to let God" is *not* inactivity, but Christ-activity—God in action accomplishing divine purposes through human personality. This never reduces our status or worth, but exalts us to the stature of a king: "Those who receive abundance of grace and of the gift of righteousness *will reign in life* through the One, Jesus Christ" (Romans 5:17).

This is not some kind of automatic sinless perfection. For it is only your faith and your obedience which allow Christ to be in you now what He was then (perfect!), and *you* will be what He was then only to the degree in which you allow *Him* to be in you what He is now (perfect!).

Return to your rest, O my soul, for the

LORD has dealt bountifully with you.

PSALM 116:7

→ How would you explain the true, biblical meaning of dying to self-effort and allowing God to work?

→ How would you describe what it truly means to experience rest in Jesus Christ?

30

Your Life a Miracle

The true life of a genuine Christian is miraculous. What defines a miracle? A miracle is something that happens for which *there is no possible explanation except God.*

The Lord Jesus reveals to us that our Christian life, if it is genuine, cannot be explained apart from Him. He says of us,

"Without Me you can do nothing" (John 15:5), as He said of Himself, "I am able to do nothing from Myself [independently, of My own accord]" (John 5:30, AMP).

What He expects of you is not the sensational or the spectacular, but simply the miraculous, which you experience by faith.

How do you walk by faith? By exposing every new situation to the Lord Jesus who, as God, lives in you through the Holy Spirit. Nothing sensational, nothing spectacular, just expose every situation to Christ: every threat, promise, opportunity, responsibility, problem, no matter what. Stand back and say, "Thank You for all of this, Lord Jesus. Thank You for what You will do so that I can live miraculously. You have been waiting for me to be available so You can live Your Life through me, which would otherwise be utterly impossible for me." Giving thanks in this way is the evidence of true faith.

The Lord Jesus Christ claims the use of *your* body, *your* whole being, *your* complete personality, so that as you give yourself to Him through the eternal Spirit, He may give Himself to you through the eternal Spirit, that all your activity as a human being on earth may be His activity in and through *you;* so that every step you take, every word you speak, everything you do, everything you are, may be an expression of the Son of God living in you. It means letting Him think through your thinking, letting Him react through your reactions, letting Him decide through your decisions.

You discover that the Life you possess as a born-again Christian is "of Him, through Him, and to Him" every moment you are here on earth.

You may be thinking, "If such a life is totally of Him, through Him, and to Him, then where do *I* come in?" You do not. That is just where you go out! This is what Paul meant when he said, "For to me, to live is Christ" (Philippians 1:21). God credits only one Person with the right to live in you, and He is Jesus Christ; so reckon yourself to be dead to all that you are *apart* from all that Christ is, and alive only unto God in all that you are, because of all that He is (Romans 6:4–11).

It is for you to *be;* it is for Him to *act.* Rest in Him, fully available to the saving Life of Christ.

Why do so few Christians enjoy this miraculous resurrection Life?

Mostly because they are educated out of it. They are taught to repudiate the indwelling presence of a risen Lord, and instead they are told to do their best for Jesus, to emulate His example, to flex their own spiritual muscles, to stand up and be counted, to clench their fists and throw out their chest.

They are taught everything except to repent and to recognize that you and I were created to be inhabited by our Maker. They are taught in prayer to beg and say "Please" instead of saying "Thank You" as they relax and rest in Christ.

Let us constantly and at all times offer up to God a sacrifice of praise, which is the fruit of lips that thankfully acknowledge and confess and glorify His name.

HEBREWS 13:15, AMP

→ In what ways have your prayers been oriented toward begging God instead of thanking Him?

→ What do you need to be thanking Him for now?

31

What Is Real Repentance?

True repentance is not being sorry for something you have done wrong. Now, if you do something wrong, you *should* be sorry; but that is not real repentance.

Real repentance is hilariously exciting. It is facing the facts of life, recognizing how God made you, how you were intended to function, and then being restored to that relationship of mutual interavailability that the Lord Jesus enjoyed between Himself and the Father, a mutual interavailability in which you are prepared to let Him be God. That is true repentance.

Repentance happens the moment you genuinely admit,

"I cannot—and only God can." Deriving from that repentance is the attitude the Bible calls *faith*. It means bowing to the fact that you cannot and only God can. It means acting on the assumption that this is true, and exposing every situation to Him moment by moment, for Him to accomplish what you cannot, while you tell Him, "Thank You!" You give Him your hands for Him to work with, your feet for Him to walk with, your lips for Him to speak with, your eyes for Him to see with, your ears for Him to hear with, your mind for Him to think with, your heart for Him to love with. You tell Him, "Thank You for being my Creator within the creature. You are in business!"

Then you begin to live miraculously. You manifest a quality of life that baffles those around you.

If, however, you do not bow to this fact that you cannot and only God can, if you do not admit it as true, this does not mean you will not continue trying to live the Christian life. The vast majority of those who are redeemed, whose names are in the Lamb's Book of Life, and who are on their way to heaven, are not prepared to act on the assumption that they cannot and only God can. They try to live the Christian life *for* Him, and they fail miserably.

When Paul in the New Testaments describes "the last days," he speaks of people "having a form of godliness but denying its power" (2 Timothy 3:1, 5), and these "last days" are the world we live in today. So many have a dead religion, destitute of what makes it functional. They are missing the hidden factor, denying the true power: God Himself. They are not letting God be God.

Faith means *letting Him.* In any particular situation you encounter, any particular need and responsibility that faces you, you will never *let Him* until you are prepared to admit that you cannot, and only God can.

O LORD my God, in You I put my trust.

PSALM 7:1

→ In what ways have you tried to live the Christian life *for* the Lord Jesus, instead of allowing Him to live it through you?

→ In growing faith, what do you need to allow the Lord to be in your life at this time?

32

What God Will Accomplish

verything God demands of us is, from God's point of view, completely logical for this simple reason: *"He who calls you is faithful, who also will do it"* (1 Thessalonians 5:24). What God demands in your life is what *He Himself will faithfully accomplish.*

Now if God has called you, and if God Himself will accomplish what He has called you to, what could possibly be illogical about anything to which He calls you?

"It is *God* who *works in you* both to will and to do for His good pleasure" (Philippians 2:13). If God has willed it, and if God Himself is going to work in you to bring about what He wills, what could possibly be illogical about any part of His will for your life?

In every demand God makes upon us, there is a hidden factor that is absent in the reasoning of fallen humanity. That hidden factor is something you should be able to guess by now: It is *God Himself.* God engineered us in such a way that the presence of the Creator within the creature is indispensable to man's humanity, so that we, in normality, will be distinguished by a quality of life and behavior that allows no possible explanation but God Himself within us.

God calls you to a life of righteousness, and by your consent He lives that life of righteousness *through* you. God calls you to go into all the world and preach the gospel to every creature, and by your consent He goes *through* you into all the world and preaches the gospel to every creature.

This is what saves us from the futility of self-effort. If you trust Christ for the Life He wants to live through you, the next step you take will be taken in the very energy and power of God Himself. You will have begun to live a life which is essentially supernatural, yet still clothed with the common humanity of your physical body.

You will have become *totally dependent* upon the Life of Christ within you, and never before will you have been so *independent,* so *emancipated* from the pressure of your circumstances and released at last from self-dependence.

You will be free from the tyranny of a defeated enemy within. You will be restored to your true humanity to be the human vehicle of the divine Life.

You must die to your own natural ability to deal with the flesh, for you cannot crucify yourself. That is God's business.

To walk in the Spirit is to have such utter confidence in Him that you first seek His instructions, then ask no further questions, but simply do as you are told. To all who do this, the promise of God is that they will not walk in the lusts of the flesh. The Holy Spirit within you is fully able to deal with your flesh and to put it and keep it in the place of death. Let Him do it!

Faithful is He Who is calling
you to Himself, and utterly trustworthy,
and He will also do it—fulfill His call
by hallowing and keeping you.

1 THESSALONIANS 5:24, AMP

→ Have you come to the place in your relationship with the Lord Jesus Christ where you have stopped questioning Him about His intentions or instructions or methods?

33

Moment-by-Moment Choices

Imagine a Christian who gets into his car, starts the engine, and drives down the road. Those actions may be no more than a series of physical acts with which his moral conscience and his moral will remain totally unconcerned until that man reaches a certain intersection where he must decide whether to turn right or left. To turn right would take him to the club where, as an alcoholic, he used to get drunk. To turn to the left would take him home to his wife and family.

Even though this man is born again, the sin principle which still operates within him will seek to dominate his natural will and to bring about decisions which enable the flesh to use his body to satisfy its carnal appetites. At the same time it will seek to silence his moral conscience and to persuade him that he can do what he wants and get away with it, with no unpleasant consequences.

Simultaneously his moral conscience, quickened and undergirded by the Holy Spirit within his human spirit, will exercise its moral will to persuade him to do what God's Word tells us to do: "Do not continue offering or yielding your bodily members and faculties to sin as instruments (tools) of wickedness. But offer and yield yourselves to God as though you have been raised from the dead to perpetual life, and your bodily members and faculties to God, presenting them as implements of righteousness" (Romans 6:13, AMP).

If the flesh is successful in silencing this man's moral conscience and in exerting its influence over his will, he will turn right at the intersection and end up at the club, morally defeated. On the other hand, if the Holy Spirit enables his moral will to exercise control over his behavior, he will turn left and arrive home to the delight of his wife and children and to the inexpressible joy of his own soul, morally victorious.

"That is just it," you may say. "Right there is where I run into trouble, right where I have to make a choice, like the man at the intersection. That is where I am beaten again and again! How can I get my natural will into harmony with my moral conscience?"

The answer lies in your attitude toward the Lord Jesus Christ and His Life which you share.

In every conflict between your moral will and the flesh regarding how your natural will is to be exercised in determining the things you think and say and do, you will say to Christ:

"Dear Lord, thank You for Your Holy Spirit. I yield my will to Him, and by His gracious presence I share Your Life and Your victory. I know I cannot overcome the principle of sin within me, nor put my flesh to death, but I thank You that You *can* and You *did*, when You died upon the cross and I died with You.

"Thank You for Your Holy Spirit, for He alone can make this real in my experience, mortifying those deeds of my body which have their origin in Satan. I am willing for You to invade my soul, to control my mind, to control my emotions, and to control my will, so that every decision within my soul will be in perfect harmony with my spirit, and my spirit in perfect harmony with You, so that my whole being may declare Your praise.

"Lord Jesus, I can't, but You can! Thank You so much."

If you are prepared to practice the presence of Christ in this way and reckon with Him through His Holy Spirit not only to keep the flesh in the place of death but to establish His divine sovereignty within every area of your soul, then you will experience that delightful transformation of character which will conform you increasingly to the image of God's dear Son.

For we walk by faith, not by sight.

2 CORINTHIANS 5:7

→ In your daily life, what does it mean to "practice the presence of Christ"?

→ What kind of moral choices in your life tend to give you the most trouble?

34

Moment of Truth

There is a moment of truth for every human soul to whom the Holy Spirit, through the human spirit, has revealed the wickedness of sin.

It is so easy to become familiar with Bible language without receiving any real revelation of truth. God wants to bring you, no matter how bitter may be the experience, to the place of self-discovery, to this moment of truth.

In startling reality, the truth as expressed by Paul may dawn upon your soul: "I am a creature of the flesh—carnal, unspiritual, having been sold into slavery under the control of sin" (Romans 7:14, AMP). This passage in Romans reveals how the human soul is exploited by the subtle principle of sin within, and clearly defines the conflict within you.

One part of you says, "I acknowledge and agree that the Law is good (morally excellent) and that I take sides with it.... I endorse and delight in the Law of God in my inmost self, with my new nature" (Romans 7:16, 22, AMP). In your human spirit, the Holy Spirit is bearing witness to all that is good and right and noble; to your enlightened moral conscience, every act and attitude of sin is an offense.

Then there is that other part of you, "the sin principle which dwells within me, fixed and operating in my soul" (Romans 7:20, AMP). You realize "that when I want to do what is right and good, evil is ever present with me and I am subject to its insistent demands" (Romans 7:21, AMP).

The moment of truth comes when you quit exchanging courtesies with the flesh and repudiate it to its face, naming it for the treacherous, wicked, worthless thing it is.

At this climactic stage in your Christian life you realize that there can be no compromise with the flesh, and that peaceful coexistence with a principle satanically hostile to the law of God and to the reestablishment of His sovereignty within your soul is now beyond the bounds of possibility.

You realize that it was never God's purpose to improve the flesh, to educate it or to tame it, let alone Christianize it. It has always been God's purpose that the flesh—condemned, sentenced, and crucified with Jesus Christ—might be left buried in the tomb and replaced by the resurrection Life of the Lord Jesus Christ Himself.

The risen Christ must exercise control in your mind, in your emotions, and in your will, expressing Himself through your personality. Paul described this clearly in his concern for the Ephesian Christians, when he prayed for them: "For this reason I bow my knees to the Father of our Lord Jesus Christ…that He would grant you, according to the riches of His glory, to be strengthened with might through His Spirit in the inner man, *that Christ may dwell in your hearts through faith*" (Ephesians 3:14–17).

You have stripped off the old unregenerate
self with its evil practices,
and have clothed yourselves with
the new spiritual self, which is ever
in the process of being renewed
and remolded into fuller and
more perfect knowledge...after the image
(the likeness) of Him Who created it.

COLOSSIANS 3:9–10, AMP

→ Have you repudiated your flesh, recognizing it and naming it for the evil and worthless thing it is? Have you fully realized that there can be no compromise with the flesh in your life?

→ How are you allowing the Lord Jesus Christ to express Himself through your personality?

35

The Privilege of Being You

Never break your heart trying to be someone else. In the first place, you never will be. You will always be *you* and no one else. The person who gets up in the morning will be the person who went to sleep the night before; so you might as well get reconciled to the fact that you are the person you are going to live with for the rest of your days.

In the second place, this is the way God wants it! He never intended that you should be anyone else, and He wants you to be the person He intended you to be.

To understand this better, have you noticed the apparent contradiction in what Jesus says about your self? He said, "If anyone desires to come after Me, let him *deny himself*" (Matthew 16:24). It becomes quite evident from this statement that there is within each of us a self to be denied, *a self to be repudiated.*

On another occasion, however, Jesus said, "You shall *love* your neighbor *as yourself*" (Matthew 22:39). If you are to love your neighbor as yourself, then you must first love yourself, or else love for your neighbor would become meaningless. It would appear therefore that there is a legitimate place for self-love. In addition to a self to be repudiated, there must be *a self to be respected.*

How then is self-respect to be reconciled with self-repudiation? Can they coexist?

The self you must repudiate is the self that the flesh makes of you when the flesh is dominant within your soul, abusing and misusing your personality.

The self you have the right to respect is the self that Christ makes of you, filling you with His Holy Spirit, enhancing and using your personality.

There is most certainly a legitimate place for healthy self-respect as a Christian, but it is the self-respect that derives from your personal relationship to Jesus Christ.

On this basis you can learn to love the most unlovely of your neighbors, because you know that if there is anything you can love or respect about yourself, it is only what Christ has made of you. Even though your neighbor lies drunk in the gutter, you can love him, not for the person that sin has made of him, but for the one you know Christ can make of him once He has taken over. You know that what Christ has made of you, He can also make of him.

You do not lose your own personality when by faith you take your place with Christ in death. On the contrary, a transformation takes place *within* your personality. You simply come under new management.

"Therefore if any person is ingrafted in Christ (the

Messiah), he is a new creation (a new creature altogether); the old, previous moral and spiritual condition has passed away. Behold, the fresh and new has come!" (2 Corinthians 5:17, AMP).

This new life which has begun is of course the Life of the Lord Jesus, and your personality becomes His means of expression. He, as God, "is all the while effectually at work in you, energizing and creating in you the power and desire, both to will and to work for His good pleasure and satisfaction and delight" (Philippians 2:13, AMP).

When you are prepared for the Lord Jesus Christ to get "in business" like that, you will not *want* to be anyone else! You will be far too excited discovering what He intends you to be.

You died, and your life is hidden with Christ in God.
COLOSSIANS 3:3

→ How do you understand the practical difference between the self you are to deny (repudiate) and the self you are to love (respect)?

→ How healthy is your self-respect? What is the basis of your self-respect?

36

Expire to Inspire

When I was a young man, I once went to a voice trainer. She was a rather large woman—not fat or flabby, just solid. I had hardly crossed the threshold into her studio when she barked at me: "Expire!"

I said, "Expire? But I'm too young!" (which I thought was incredibly funny). She did not think so, and she made it demonstrably obvious that she did not think so.

So I expired.

"That is *not* the way to expire," she quickly told me. She then showed me the proper way to do it, and man, could she expire! *Whooo-ooo-ooo-ooo!* By the time she was through expiring, she seemed to be about half her former size.

Then she barked at me again: "Inspire!"

So I inspired.

She said, "That is not the way to inspire." She expired again, then inspired—and man, did she inspire! She sucked so hard I thought the pictures would come off the wall. I could almost see the grand piano coming across the room, and her mouth seemed open wide enough to swallow it.

She then preached to me a magnificent sermon. "You will

never, ever learn to *in*spire," she said, "until first you have learned to *ex*pire; otherwise, you will only *per*spire!"

Is that not good?

To be crucified with Christ is to be executed judicially with Him, to *expire*. To those who expire in this way, God has given the very Life that He restored to the Lord Jesus when He raised Him from the dead, so that we can say not only, "I have been crucified with Christ," but also, "It is no longer I who live, but Christ (the Messiah) lives in me" (Galatians 2:20, AMP). That is to *inspire*.

With every step we take into the future, we can say, "With Christ I died, and now through Him I live, as He shares His Life with me on earth on my way to heaven, and then forever."

That is what it means to be a Christian.

With every step you take, you first expire: "Lord Jesus, *I can't;* You never said I could."

Then you inspire: "Lord Jesus, *You can,* and always said You would!"

This is what keeps you from the futility of doing nothing more than perspire.

For if we have been united together in the likeness of His death, certainly we also shall be in the likeness of His resurrection.

ROMANS 6:5

➔ What does it mean to you to "expire" as well as to "inspire"?

37

The Complete Answer

The Christians of the early church have been described as being "incorrigibly happy, completely unafraid, and nearly always in trouble."

That is gloriously true, and Paul gives us an illustration of this attitude in the second epistle to the Corinthians when he was in a situation that was beyond human endurance. "We were burdened beyond measure," he says, "...so that we despaired even of life."

Then he goes on, "Yes, we had the sentence of death in ourselves, that *we should not trust in ourselves but in God* who raises the dead" (2 Corinthians 1:8-9). He was adopting this attitude: Our present difficulty is not our problem; it is *His* problem. It is in the hands of our God, who raises the dead.

Here was Paul dying to self, and this dying to self allowed him to hand the whole situation over to the One indwelling him, Jesus Christ, the God of resurrection power.

Dying to self is a wonderful position to be in, because dead people cannot die, and dead people do not have problems.

You see, every time you give yourself the right to have a problem or the right to worry about something, you give yourself the right to live your own life. However, if you adopt an attitude of total dependence on the Life of the Lord Jesus, the only life with which God will ever credit you, then no matter how threatening a situation may be, you can relate it to Him. You can say, "Thank You, Lord! This is no longer my problem or my worry; it is *Yours.*"

This is the quality of life that gives you "the peace of God that passes all understanding." It is the quality of life that staggers your neighbors, leaving them perplexed and baffled as they see you remain on such an even keel in situations which would completely demoralize them.

This is the privilege that is yours and mine in Jesus Christ. It applies to every single situation in life without exception, to every decision you may be confronted with today, to every temptation that faces you, and to every responsibility you may be called upon to carry. This truth always applies: The Lord Jesus, the God of resurrection Life, indwells you bodily with all the adequacy of the Godhead, "and you are *complete* in Him" (Colossians 2:10).

I love Paul's thoughts in Philippians 4:13 in *The Amplified Bible:* "I am ready for anything and equal to anything through Him Who infuses inner strength into me; I am self-sufficient in Christ's sufficiency." Paul needed no crutches, because through dependence on Christ's completeness and competency he himself was completely competent.

To be wholly and completely and exclusively dependent on Christ's competence—that is the Christian Life. It is not just the monopoly of the few, nor is it the privilege only of God's special favorites. It is the Life for which *you* were redeemed. Christ's precious blood was shed to reconcile you to God, so that Christ, now risen from the dead, might share His resurrection Life with you.

It does not mean you will avoid pressures and threats and discomforts, but you can know that in every situation you have the complete, total, and absolute answer…in Christ, your Life. *He* is the answer.

To live a life less than this is to miss the whole point of your redemption.

I can do all things through Christ who strengthens me.

PHILIPPIANS 4:13

→ For what current problems in particular have you been giving yourself the "right" to worry? How instead can you relate each of these situations to God, and release them to His responsibility?

→ What specific decisions or responsibilities are you now facing that need to be entrusted into God's hands?

→ By genuinely depending on Christ's sufficiency, what challenges in your life are you truly competent to face? Express your gratitude to Him for all of this.

38

What You Know or Don't Know

To be the kind of Christian God truly wants you to be, you do not need a theological degree. You do not have to be all that smart, or unusually endowed with some special gift. Of course, you should not despise anything with which God has endowed you, and you should be profoundly thankful for any and all of it. Bear in mind, however, that His activity in your humanity will never be limited or determined by any particular gift or skill you may possess.

The only limitation on what God can do in you and in

me is our availability. Be available to Christ, and His divine dynamic will be released.

Nearly five centuries ago, the German theologian and reformer Johann Bugenhagen expressed it very succinctly: If you really know the Lord Jesus personally, then what you *do not* know does not really matter; but if you do not know the Lord Jesus personally, whatever you *do* know is worth nothing.

No matter how unimportant we may feel ourselves to be, we can pulsate with the divine energy and have an unshatterable confidence that Christ is in action as we personally depend upon Him.

In such a relationship, the lovely thing is that He does not have to tell us what He is doing. All we need to know is that He is doing it. Sometimes for our joy or His own purposes He does tell us, but He may wait years to reveal to us the incredible consequences of what He has done.

That is what makes life so incredibly exciting to me, and increasingly more so as the years go by.

The Christian life is not about our own capacity and ability, but about God's; not about who we are, but who He is; not about what we have to offer, but what He offers, which is all of Himself, if only we are as available to Christ as Christ was available to His Father.

All of the Father was available to all of the Son, because by His faith-love relationship, all of the Son was available to all of the Father; this is what constituted His perfect Manhood. In the same way, the availability of the Son to *you* will be experienced to the degree of your availability to the

Son, because of your faith-love relationship to Him.

All that God *gives,* which is all that you *need,* He gives to you in Christ, "that no flesh should glory in His presence. But of Him you are in Christ Jesus, who became for us wisdom from God—and righteousness and sanctification and redemption" (1 Corinthians 1:29–30).

The God who commanded light to shine out of darkness...has shone in our hearts to give the light of the knowledge of the glory of God in the face of Jesus Christ.

2 CORINTHIANS 4:6

→ How would you assess the degree of your availability to Christ? Are you placing any limitations on what the Lord can do through you?

→ How are you learning more profoundly that in Christ God gives you everything you need?

39

Hanging in the Balance

A moment comes in the life of every child of God when God's purpose for your life hangs delicately in the balance. Fulfillment will come only with the realization that you do not have in yourself what it takes. Death to all that you are in your own inadequacy is the only gateway through which you may enter into the fullness of all that Christ is, so that you may live miraculously in the power of His resurrection, crying out from the heart, "Lord Jesus, I cannot—but *You can,* and that is all I need to know. Let's go!"

In the Bible, when Esther agreed to risk her life by going to the Persian king to plead for the deliverance of God's people, she said, "If I perish, I perish" (Esther 4:16). Her response was both crisp and courageous, and it presents a picture of true discipleship that is thrilling and dramatic.

The issue she faced was final and embraced all lesser issues. Esther now was alive to God alone and dead to self and all self-interest. Compelled, as though by some unseen, inner thrust, Esther threw her life away.

When Esther made her crucial decision, she resolved to

fast for three days and nights before going to the king. Three days and nights—does that remind you of anything?

Willingness to die is the price you must pay if you want to be raised from the dead to live and work and walk in the power of the third morning, sharing the resurrection Life of Jesus Christ, the One who said He would be "three days and three nights in the heart of the earth" (Matthew 12:40), and who promised that after He was crucified He would "be raised the third day" (Matthew 16:21).

Once the willingness to die is there for us, there are no more issues to face, only instructions to obey.

Pass the sentence of death upon yourself, even as Esther did, and you can afford to do as you are told.

Jesus both shows us and teaches us about this sentence of death:

> I assure you, most solemnly I tell you, unless a grain
> of wheat falls into the earth and dies, it remains just
> one grain; it never becomes more but lives by itself
> alone. But if it dies, it produces many others and
> yields a rich harvest.
>
> JOHN 12:24, AMP

On the particular occasion when those words were spoken, Jesus was referring initially to Himself. He was that sinless, spotless grain of wheat planted by the Father at Calvary. But He was also speaking about us.

Unless we are prepared to die, we will never become what we were intended to be.

Dead men cannot die, nor can they be frightened, and responsibility does not rest too heavily upon their shoulders. In fact, there is nothing quite so relaxing as being dead—dead, I mean, to your own ability to accomplish anything apart from Jesus Christ.

To many pragmatic minds, this total repudiation of self-effort is abhorrent. The thought of it can result in a hostility borne of self-justification. Such people often are very dedicated in their desire to serve God, but they are baffled by the whole concept of a Christian life which is nothing more nor less than Jesus Christ Himself in action.

You can afford to die, however, once you see clearly and become utterly convinced that death to yourself means trading what *you* are for what *Christ* is.

At this point, unbelief so often rears its ugly head. If you are not wholly convinced that Jesus Christ is willing and able to take over, you will hang on desperately to whatever you think you are in yourself. If you keep hanging on, you can be absolutely certain you will never know the profound peace that comes from allowing the Lord Jesus Christ to assume responsibility for your life.

I beseech you therefore, brethren, by the mercies of God, that you present your bodies a living sacrifice, holy, acceptable to God, which is your reasonable service. And do not be conformed to this world, but be transformed by the renewing of your mind, that you may prove what is that good and acceptable and perfect will of God.

→ In what ways have you been hanging on to whatever you think you are in yourself?

→ Do you have a full willingness to die to self?

→ Have you become clearly and utterly convinced that death to yourself means trading what *you* are for what *Christ* is?

40

Faith Is Like a Clutch

f you have received the Lord Jesus Christ as your Savior and have become a child of God, it will be the constant delight of the Holy Spirit to seek your health and welfare and to speak peace to your soul.

An important lesson to learn, however, is the amazing fact that in spite of His omnipotence, God limits Himself in His relationship to each of us by the law of faith. Though the Holy Spirit inhabits your humanity, representing both the Father and the Son, He will never violate the sovereignty of your will nor deprive you of your moral responsibility to choose.

Though He is God Himself, the Holy Spirit has chosen always to govern your behavior and exercise supreme control in every part of your being *only by your own free choice and glad consent.*

It is this power of veto, this right to choose, which lifts you out of the animal kingdom and makes you the moral being that God created man to be. It is this and only this which enables you to love God and reciprocate His love for you.

That is why your free "yes" to God, at any given moment, fills His heart with greater joy than all the thrilling wonders of a million universes thrown out into the vastness of outer space by the word of His power. Nothing else in creation has the capacity to love Him, because nothing else has the capacity to choose Him.

The privilege of being you is that you can know God and love God *for yourself!*

In such a relationship, faith is like the clutch in a car with manual transmission.

Imagine a young driver in a convertible sports car, with a friend at his side, as he takes off down the highway, shifting through the gears, then zooming along at seventy, eighty, ninety miles per hour (no police in sight).

With the wind blowing through his hair, the driver turns to his friend and says, "Man, what a clutch!"

Is that what he would say?

Of course not. He would say, "Man, what an engine!" All that the clutch does is to enable the driver to engage the power under the hood and apply it to the wheels on the road.

Sometimes we say, "What a man of faith!" or "What a woman of faith!" Never congratulate people on their faith, however, because in itself faith does nothing. If people exercise faith and anything marvelous happens, it is not *because* of that faith; their faith is only the clutch. The activity that is released through our faith is God's, and *He* is to be congratulated. He is the power under the hood.

132

*Now faith is the assurance
(the confirmation, the title deed)
of the things we hope for, being the
proof of things we do not see and
the conviction of their reality—
faith perceiving as real fact what is
not revealed to the senses.*

→ Are you by faith turning to God by your free choice
and glad consent?

→ What growth are you experiencing in personally loving
God?

41

The Law of Faith

od's sovereignty is absolutely unchallengeable. He is *God!* He can do anything He pleases, but the incredible thing is this: In order to have in each of us a creature who can love Him in return, He in His unchallengeable sovereignty has deliberately chosen to limit the exercise of that sovereignty in the option He has given to human beings. That is why you and I have been granted the greatest liberty possible, that of exercising the disposition of our choice toward the God who created us.

God brings us to the conviction that the Word of God is true, but then He waits until we respond with "the obedience of faith" (Romans 16:26, KJV). It is true that our faith is created and cherished and nourished by God Himself, for "faith comes by hearing, and hearing by the word of God" (Romans 10:17), but our faith is inoperative until we yield *obedience* to the faith God has produced.

In other words, we mix His Word with the obedience of faith, then He moves into action and demonstrates the glorious truth of His Word. Otherwise we are like those disobedient persons described in Hebrews 4:2: "For indeed the gospel was preached to us as well as to them; but the word which they heard did not profit them, *not being mixed with faith* in those who heard it."

You must *act* on what you have come to know and believe before it will ever become real in your experience, before you realize by personal experience that Jesus is alive not just in heaven but in *you* every moment of every day, as the Father was alive in Him. Then your actions will be the activity of faith.

Without faith, you cannot do what only Christ can do. You end up a dead loss. *With* faith, you allow Christ to do through you what only He can do.

Faith is the law that governs our relationship to God and God's relationship to us. Just as God has designed a rigid interlock between the instinctive thrust and the animal soul, so faith is the moral interlock between the Holy Spirit and the human soul, to establish our love for God, in dependence on God, through our total obedience to God.

That threefold moral relationship allows God to accomplish His will in you and through you. He does it one step at a time, in every new situation into which that step takes you.

Faith on your part invites and invokes Christ's activity; for without your faith and this moral relationship, He would be violating your humanity. He would be treating you like an animal that *must* do what instinct commands by the law of compulsion. You and I, however, were created to act and respond on the basis of a law of love. In love and dependence and obedience, we let *Him* do it.

This is what it means to walk by faith, in the Spirit, and

this is what satisfies God. Some mechanical conformity to religious demands that squeezes you into a religious strait-jacket can never satisfy God. What satisfies Him is to see you, in every situation, bowing yourself out and bowing Him in, and saying, "God, I believe exactly what You have told me. Without You I am nothing, have nothing, and can do nothing, for the only way I can please You is by faith. I let *You* do it. Thank You!"

Then life becomes a miracle.

> *Without having seen Him, you love Him;*
> *though you do not even now see Him,*
> *you believe in Him and exult and*
> *thrill with inexpressible and glorious*
> *(triumphant, heavenly) joy.*
>
> 1 PETER 1:8, AMP

→ How are you inviting and invoking Christ's activity in your life by faith? What does this mean practically?

→ How are you seeing that your life is a miracle, as you please God by faith?

42

How Much Can Jesus Do?

The moment you dare to say, "I am a Christian, I am a member of the Body of Christ, I share His Life who is the Head of that Body, and I am solely and totally available to Him"—from that moment, you have no further right to please yourself.

Of course, from the world's point of view, in their denial or ignorance of God, you always have the right to insist on pleasing yourself. As a Christian, however, you no longer have that; you have signed it away forever.

We are "not to please ourselves," Paul says. "For *even Christ did not please Himself*" (Romans 15:1–3).

Even Christ! We may wonder, "Does not God have the right to please Himself?" As God, yes; but fulfilling the role of Man, never—and that which was true of Jesus in His humanity is also true for us in our restored humanity.

That seems tough, does it not? This is real Christianity, however. What God had in mind in sending His Son was to restore us to the quality of life that derives from the presence of the Creator within the creature.

This is how Jesus lived, so that He said of His Father, "I always do those things that please Him" (John 8:29). He was showing us our true humanity, because *we were created to* *please God.* "But without faith it is impossible to please Him" (Hebrews 11:6). We were created to please God, yet without faith it is impossible to do so. Therefore what do we discover about faith? That it is not an option; it is not a luxury; it is not a personal point of view. It is an *imperative* and an absolute necessity for our humanity.

How much then can Jesus Christ do through you and through me as we live by such faith?

Anything and everything. God is limited only by the measure of our availability to all that He makes available to us, for "in Him dwells all the fullness of the Godhead bodily; and you are complete in Him" (Colossians 2:9–10).

What is it, then, that releases divine activity into our lives? This is the critical question of Christian experience, and the answer is simple: "The just shall live by faith" (Romans 1:17). Faith in all its sheer simplicity. Childlike faith that takes God precisely at His Word. Faith that simply says, "Thank You, dear Lord."

If you are to know the fullness of Life in Christ, you are to appropriate the efficacy *of what He is* as you have already appropriated the efficacy of *what He has done*. Relate everything, moment by moment as it arises, to the adequacy of *what He is in you,* and assume that His adequacy will be operative. On this basis you are exhorted to "rejoice always" (1 Thessalonians 5:16). You are to be incorrigibly cheerful, for you have solid grounds upon which to rejoice.

Can any situation possibly arise, under any circumstances, for which the Lord Jesus is less than adequate? Any pressure, promise, problem, responsibility, or temptation? If He be truly God, not one!

That being so, applying His adequacy by faith to every situation as it arises will leave you with no alternative but to obey this injunction: "In everything give thanks" (1 Thessalonians 5:18). In how many things? In *everything* without exception, for "this is the will of God in Christ Jesus for you." If in any situation you are not prepared to give thanks, you are out of the will of God.

> *Christ…was raised from the dead in order*
>
> *that we may bear fruit for God.*
>
> ROMANS 7:4, AMP

→ In what ways have you seen that you still try to please yourself in life?

→ What is it that releases God's activity in your life?

→ In what problems and difficulties in your life have you seen the adequacy of the Lord Jesus, as you have relied on Him?

43

Is Sinless Perfection Possible?

You may be wondering, "Is my old, sinful nature wholly eradicated the moment I claim by faith my identity with Christ in death?"

There is no climactic experience by which the evil influence of the flesh may be eradicated once and for all, though the flesh itself in its subtlety would like you to believe it, in the interests of its own self-preservation. If you are persuaded that the flesh no longer exists, you are not likely to cause it any further inconvenience as it perpetuates its wicked activities in your soul. Nothing could please the devil more!

Appropriation of the victory of Christ demands more than just one act of faith. It requires an *attitude* of faith. It is a moment-by-moment reckoning, and your reckoning for this moment is never adequate for the next. A continuous attitude is required, a step-by-step forward walk: "Walk in the Spirit, and you shall not fulfill the lust of the flesh" (Galatians 5:16). You must reckon *positively* with the Holy Spirit in every new situation you encounter, to keep the flesh in the place of death.

I emphasize *positively* because we are to reckon ourselves not only "to be dead indeed to sin," but also to be "alive to God in Christ Jesus our Lord" (Romans 6:11). Our enjoyment of the resurrection Life of the Lord Jesus Christ, through reckoning positively with His presence, is that which sets us free from the law of sin and death. The surest way of reckoning yourself to be dead to sin (that old Adamic nature) is to reckon yourself alive in Jesus Christ and to be utterly dependent upon Him. He then will take care of the consequences.

In such a life, is sinless perfection possible?

If to walk in the Spirit, in moment-by-moment dependence upon Him, is *not* to fulfill the lusts of the flesh, as Paul clearly states in Galatians 5:16, then the converse is equally true: *Not* to walk in the Spirit means that you will fall prey to the lusts of the flesh.

The Bible presents an overwhelming case for Christian victory *as long as we are prepared to fulfill the conditions and appropriate by faith the victorious Life of Christ Himself.* On the other hand, nowhere in the Bible is there any support for the promise of sinless perfection, except on that wonderful day when we shall see the Lord Jesus Christ face-to-face. Then indeed "we shall be like Him, for we shall see Him as He is" (1 John 3:2).

Do not allow anyone therefore to deceive you about this, for this will only lead you into dishonesty, no matter how sincere you may be, as you seek to reconcile a bad conscience with your claim to sinless perfection. You will simply have to invent some other name for sin while you pretend that sin does not exist.

The Holy Spirit is your Comforter and Friend; as such, He will be faithful to convict you of sin. He is within you to keep you from falling, so be very sensitive to all He has to say to you.

When the Holy Spirit names it, call it by its name! Admit and confess it for the sin that it is. Claim instantly the cleansing that God has promised through the death and resurrection of Christ, for "the blood of Jesus Christ His Son cleanses us from all sin" (1 John 1:7), and be thankful that the Holy Spirit in residence within you is constantly alert and ready instantly to expose wickedness and evil.

If we say we have no sin, refusing to admit that we are sinners, we delude and lead ourselves astray, and the Truth which the Gospel presents is not in us (does not dwell in our hearts).

1 JOHN 1:8, AMP

→ What is your understanding of the biblical answer to this question: Is sinless perfection possible in your life on earth?

→ What does it mean practically to reckon ourselves to be dead to sin and alive to God in Christ Jesus (as taught in Romans 6:11)?

→ What is the biblical basis for experiencing victory over sin in our lives?

44

When Your Work Is Spoiled

The story is told of a famous artist who was painting a mural beneath the dome of a great cathedral. One day he and an assistant were standing on a working platform built under the dome, and the artist was admiring his work. It seemed incredibly beautiful to him, and he was intoxicated by what he had achieved with his genius and ability. He could not take his eyes off his own masterpiece.

To take it all in to better advantage, he slowly took a step backward, then another, and another, until one step further would plunge him to his death on the stone floor far below.

His assistant saw what has happening. With amazing presence of mind, he took the bucket of paint he was holding and threw it over the mural.

Stopping in his tracks, the artist cried out in anger, "You have spoiled my picture!"

"Yes sir," his assistant replied, "but I saved your life! You will live to paint again."

It may well seem to you at times that God has spoiled your "picture"—all that you hoped to accomplish with your own talent and gifting, your own great ideas, success, and performance. You resent what He has allowed to happen, but the Holy Spirit will quietly say, "Yes indeed, I spoiled your picture, but I saved your life! You will live to paint again, but the hand that holds the brush will be the hand of God!"

If you have received the Lord Jesus Christ as your Redeemer, if the Holy Spirit has come to take up residence within your human spirit and you have been born again, and yet that old, Adamic nature, the flesh, still dominates your soul and monopolizes your personality by coloring your thinking, sparking your ambitions, capturing your affections, and subtly persuading your will into submission to its claims upon you, then you are a carnal Christian. You are what the New Testament describes as a mere baby in Christ, and the Holy Spirit is grieved by your immaturity.

Are you bewildered about your Christian experience? You know you are redeemed, but beneath the outward practice and profession of your faith you are conscious of the inner nagging of a troubled spirit. True inner peace eludes you, and you sigh for release. Perhaps like many others you have said to yourself, "I need a new church home, a new spiritual environment."

If you try out yet another new church, all that will happen is that you will simply encounter as much trouble as you found in the last one. There is nothing wrong with your spiritual environment, but there is something desperately wrong with you. If you fail to correct that, you will be a spiritual tramp all the days of your life.

Remember again this essential fact: How much can you do without Christ? Nothing. Jesus said, "The Son can do nothing of Himself," and to us He says, "without Me you can do nothing" (John 5:19; 15:5). It is astonishing, however, how busy we can be doing nothing!

"The flesh," everything that you do apart from Him, "profits nothing" (John 6:63), and there is always the awful possibility, if you do not discover this principle, that you may spend a lifetime in the service of Jesus Christ *doing nothing*. That, above everything else, we must seek to avoid.

God...gives life to the dead.

ROMANS 4:17

→ Have you experienced bewilderment about your Christian experience? Are you conscious of the inner nagging of a troubled spirit? If so, what do you believe is the reason for this, from God's perspective?

→ Could there be immaturity in your Christian life which is grieving the Holy Spirit?

45

Evangelically House-Trained

There are countless thousands of young people who profess to be Christians and whose conduct conforms to certain patterns that are prescribed within the evangelical culture. They follow such behavior not because they have any deep spiritual conviction in these matters, but simply because they have been evangelically house-trained. As they grow older and go off to a secular university or into the armed forces or into some other environment that detaches them from the evangelical mold to which they have been conformed, the results are inevitably disastrous. Confronted with the cold facts of life in a world of vastly different standards, they discover that they never had any real conscience about anything; they simply did what made them acceptable to the particular religious group they adhered to at the time.

They were following a *conscience of convenience* that governs behavior according to what is *consequentially* right or wrong.

A *conscience of conviction,* on the other hand, determines what is *morally* right or wrong. While the conscience of convenience is subject to every changing wind of fashion, the conscience of conviction, under the full control of the Holy Spirit, is anchored in truth. When the Holy Spirit comes to take up residence within the spirit of a human being, He brings with Him those absolute standards of righteousness which reflect the very nature and character of God Himself.

When the Holy Spirit begins to reveal to your human spirit the naked wickedness of your flesh, such distressing conviction may cause you to wonder whether you were ever really saved. This is a healthy symptom, and one of the surest evidences of genuine spiritual new birth.

The Holy Spirit's work is like carrying a lamp into a dark and dirty room; something you have learned to live with in the dark suddenly becomes repugnant when seen in the light.

It is always an ugly experience when the Holy Spirit introduces you to the true nature of your flesh, ripping the mask from its repulsive face. You feel you want to flee and weep bitterly, as Peter did (Luke 22:62). You realize how much you need a deeper work of grace than simply a transaction that gets you out of hell and into heaven. Out of the bitterness of self-discovery you begin to cry out as David did:

> Behold, I was brought forth in iniquity, and in sin my mother conceived me. Behold, You desire truth in the inward parts.... Hide Your face from my sins, and blot out all my iniquities. Create in me a clean heart, O God, and renew a steadfast spirit within me. Do not cast me away from Your presence, and do not take Your Holy Spirit from me.
>
> PSALM 51:5–6, 9–11

And you will find the joy that David experienced: "I will bless the LORD at all times; His praise shall continually be in my mouth" (Psalm 34:1).

Repent (change your mind and purpose); turn around and return to God, that your sins may be erased (blotted out, wiped clean), that times of refreshing (of recovering from the effects of heat, of reviving with fresh air) may come from the presence of the Lord.

ACTS 3:19, AMP

- For what sins in your life is the Holy Spirit bringing conviction?

- What standards of righteousness is the Holy Spirit emphasizing to your conscience?

46

An Awakening Soul

The familiar story in John 9 about the man born blind whom Jesus healed illustrates in a beautiful way the Holy Spirit's ministry of awakening the soul.

When the formerly blind man was repeatedly questioned about how he was healed, he unashamedly explained to them what Jesus had done. Was this man a Christian at that point? No. He did not know enough to be a Christian. He did not know how his sins could be forgiven through the shed blood of our incarnate Savior. He did not know what it means to receive God's gift of Himself through the person of the Holy Spirit and be restored to that spiritual state of Life in which man was created to function. The expression "born again" meant nothing to him, but he knew that a Man called Jesus had broken into his life.

When he tried to explain this to the Pharisees, they turned the whole thing into a theological debate as cold and icy as academic Christianity so often is today. As they questioned him again about Jesus, he boldly answered, "He is a prophet" (John 9:17). Did that make him a Christian? No, but there was clearly an awakening within his soul.

As the controversy continued, the man said something to the Pharisees that was like waving a red rag to a bull. He asked them, "Do you also want to become His disciples?" (John 9:27).

The Pharisees then "reviled him" (John 9:28), and the man quietly began to preach to them. He concluded with this incisive observation: "If this Man were not from God, He could do nothing" (John 9:33). In other words, "This is nothing less than *God at work*"—exactly what the Lord Jesus had set out to demonstrate. This man was an awakening soul but not yet a Christian; he had not yet come to that moment of moral option where he had to make a choice, to say yes or no to Christ.

The Pharisees quickly got their fill of preaching from the man who had been blind, and "they cast him out" (John 9:34).

The Lord Jesus then broke into the man's life again. Jesus knew that before anyone can be spiritually reborn, there must be an awakening of the soul whereby we know what we need and are then humble enough to admit it and receive what only God can give. So finding this man, He asked him, "Do you believe in the Son of God?" The man answered, "Who is He, Lord, that I may believe in Him?" (John 9:35–36). He was saying, "If He is a friend of Yours, He is a friend of mine; if this Son of God is the One who makes You the kind of man You are, I cannot wait to get to know Him too."

Jesus told him, "You have both seen Him and it is He who is talking with you" (John 9:37).

Then came the moment of decision for the man born blind, for this statement from Jesus demanded a moral response. At once the man answered, "Lord, I believe!" We know he genuinely recognized the truth about Jesus because immediately "he worshiped Him" (John 9:38). He had seen God at work, and now he acknowledged that the Man called Jesus was God incarnate.

When an awakened soul is adequately instructed and is prepared to yield in "the obedience of faith" (Romans 16:26, KJV), that is when God acts to regenerate that soul. In that moment you look Jesus in the face and say, "Now I know enough and believe enough for You to reconcile me, and to receive me and seal me by the Holy Spirit as Your child forever, indwelt by the Life of Christ."

Awake, you who sleep, arise from the dead, and Christ will give you light.

EPHESIANS 5:14

→ What persons around you do you recognize as "awakening souls," those who are recognizing their need for what only God can give?

47

Enabling Others to Meet Jesus Through Us

You and I are always, twenty-four hours a day, in the business of evangelism, as we allow the Lord Jesus to clothe His Deity with our humanity so that others can meet the Man called Jesus *in us.*

That is why you can never help people understand faith in Jesus simply by listing for them all the big things you are doing on His behalf. These are only evidence of the faith you have in yourself.

The true Christian life can be explained only in terms of Jesus Christ, and if your life as a Christian can still be explained in terms of *you*—your personality, your willpower, your gifts, your talents, your money, your courage, your scholarship, your dedication, your sacrifice, or your anything—then although you may have the Christian life, you are not yet living it.

If your life as a Christian can be explained in terms of you, what have you to offer to your neighbor next door? The way he lives his life can already be explained in terms of *him*, and as far as he is concerned, the only difference between him and you is that you happen to be "religious" while he is not. "Christianity" may be your hobby, but not his, and there is nothing about the way you practice it which strikes him as at all remarkable. There is nothing about you which leaves him guessing, and nothing commendable of which he does not feel himself equally capable without the inconvenience of becoming a Christian.

Only when your quality of life baffles your neighbors are you likely to get their attention. It must become patently obvious to them that the kind of life you are living is not only commendable, but beyond all human explanation. Your life must be the consequence only of God's capacity to reproduce Himself in you, however little they may understand this. The people around you must become convinced that the Lord Jesus Christ is Himself the essential ingredient of the life you live.

We are surrounded by seeking souls whom the Holy Spirit, in all kinds of wonderful ways, has been awakening so that they may become conscious of the missing factor in their existence—even though they probably will not be able to rationalize that need or put it into words. That missing factor is God Himself, and without Him, human life is only mere existence.

So be alert and sensitive to the One indwelling your humanity. He is watching all over the world, looking not on the outside but on the inside of those around you. "The LORD looks at the heart" (1 Samuel 16:7), and their awakening hearts are longing to see the reality of God in you.

The love of Christ compels us.

2 CORINTHIANS 5:14

✢   Are those around you baffled by what God is doing in your life?

✢   Who are the seeking souls around you?

48

A Young Boy's Witness

After World War II, as our new ministry was growing in England, we had thousands of young Germans who came and took part. We called them "Torchbearers" ("*Fackletraeger*"). One of them was a delightful boy whom we called Hubie, whose father had died in the war in the German army. Hubie came into my study one day and we prayed together and he received Jesus Christ. Afterwards he was insatiable in his appetite for the Lord.

When he returned to Germany, he was diagnosed with Hodgkin's disease. The doctors gave him only a matter of weeks to live, but in the goodness of God he was kept alive for some five years, a good part of which was spent in our home. Though he was often quite tired and sometimes had to be hospitalized, at other times he was able to be active, and he had one ambition: to lead someone else to Christ.

One Sunday during those years, I spoke to Jean, a Belgian boy who was visiting, and asked him to join us for the Lord's Supper which we would be observing that morning.

"No," Jean replied, "I could not do that." He explained

that he had discovered, since coming to us, that he was not a Christian.

I did not have time to talk further with him at that moment, but when I saw Hubie a few minutes later, I told him what Jean had said and asked him to look out for him.

That afternoon, Hubie came to me grinning from ear to ear, and told me he had talked with Jean, and the boy was now born again. Then Hubie told me this: "I am so thankful to God for this, because ever since I became a Christian I have asked God to make me a blessing to a Belgian boy. You see, it was a Belgian in the Resistance who shot my father dead. I want to repay a Belgian boy with the gift of life, for what a German boy suffered from the death of his dad."

Who did that Belgian boy meet in the humanity of a dying German youth with only a year or two to live? Not Hubie, but the Man called Jesus.

That is evangelism, twenty-four hours a day, so that those who rub shoulders with you, whenever and wherever, will meet the Man called Jesus as their soul begins to awaken. In a thousand and one ways you and I can communicate that there is Somebody dwelling within us, and He reigns.

The greatest single contribution you can make to those around you—your friends and your family—is that they should recognize in you the Man called Jesus, through all that you do and say and are, and even by the look on your face and the tone of your voice.

That is evangelism.

If what this book explains is really true, and all this is not just some fantasy, some noble ideal, if Christ Himself as a person actually lives inside you and me in the power of His resurrection, then what should others legitimately and logically expect from us? What kind of activity should they anticipate?

The answer is this: Nothing less than the behavior of Christ Himself.

The first chapter of the book of Genesis tells us that God made two great lights and set them in the firmament of the heavens, a greater light (the sun) to rule the day, and a lesser light (the moon) to rule the night.

The moon, however, is lightless of itself. It shines into the darkness only by virtue of its relationship to the greater light, the sun. It has nothing of itself to offer a world in the dark; it has only the sunlight that it receives and faithfully reflects, just as we have only the light of the Lord, and nothing of our own, to offer the world of darkness around us.

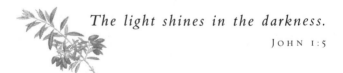

The light shines in the darkness.

JOHN 1:5

✦ Are others recognizing in you the Man called Jesus, through all that you do and say and are?

49

Going Where You
Are Sent

The incredible privilege God has given to you and to
me is to be told what to do and to do as we are told.
We can have hilarious expectation of that, because
God knows what He is about and has all that it takes to
accomplish His divine objectives. Our life becomes the
incredible adventure of being caught up into His eternal, saving purpose.

In the book of Acts, after Stephen was stoned and the
church was persecuted and scattered, the deacon named
Philip "went down to the city of Samaria and preached Christ
to them" (Acts 8:5). The impact was immediate and amazing:
"The multitudes with one accord heeded the things spoken
by Philip, hearing and seeing the miracles which he did. For
unclean spirits, crying with a loud voice, came out of many
who were possessed; and many who were paralyzed and lame
were healed. And there was great joy in that city" (Acts
8:6–8). Philip the deacon had become Philip the evangelist,
Philip the great citywide crusader.

Soon, however, "an angel of the Lord spoke to Philip, saying, 'Arise and go toward the south along the road which goes down from Jerusalem to Gaza.' *This is desert"* (Acts 8:26). This angel of the Lord, representing, of course, the Lord Jesus, was simply communicating His instructions to a healthy member of His Body: "Arise and go into the desert." There were no further instructions.

We might expect Philip to argue: "I am Philip the evangelist! Don't You remember what happened in Samaria when I preached in that city? What do You expect me to do in the desert, preach to a bunch of goats?"

Philip did not argue, however, because he was a man being filled with the Holy Spirit. How do we know? Because immediately after Philip received his instructions, "he arose and went" (Acts 8:27). When you are sent and you go, you are put where Christ puts you, and nothing will frighten you.

That is why these early believers earned the reputation of being incorrigibly happy, utterly unafraid, and nearly always in trouble.

You know what happened next to Philip. On that same desert road was another traveler, an Ethiopian eunuch whose soul was awakening. He had been to the temple in Jerusalem where he expected to hear how he could find God, but there was nobody there to tell him. So he was going home empty-hearted, but God did not leave him in the lurch. He sent him Philip, a healthy member of His Body who welcomed the incredible adventure of doing what he was told.

No one walking the roads and streets of our neighborhoods today will meet the Lord Jesus in His own body, but

He indeed does have a body on earth at this time. You and I are the hands, feet, lips, eyes, ears, mind, and heart of Jesus Christ. We are here to advertise Deity.

Ours are the only bodies on earth He has, but through them our fellow human beings can receive a physical, visible, and audible expression of the glory of the invisible God.

Christ was sentenced, executed, and buried, but now, risen, He has come to live within you and me. With our hands, some little child can feel His touch. Through our lips, some desperately lonely woman can hear His voice, and a frightened man running away from life, crushed by circumstances, can look us in the face and see Christ smile.

So we pray: "Restore me, dear Lord, to function. I do not deserve it, and you never said I did, but I want You within me to have what only You deserve—the right to be God in a man."

Go therefore and make disciples of all the nations, baptizing them in the name of the Father and of the Son and of the Holy Spirit.

MATTHEW 28:19

→ Are you prepared to "arise and go" immediately when God's call comes?

→ How have you experienced the confidence and fearlessness of knowing you were fully in God's will?

50

Arise and Go

rise and go" was the Lord's command to Philip in Acts 8, and in the next chapter another healthy member of Christ's body on earth hears that same command for a new situation: "Arise and go to the street called Straight, and inquire at the house of Judas for one called Saul of Tarsus, for behold, he is praying" (Acts 9:11).

This call was more disturbing than Philip's instructions to go into the desert. Ananias could not help but wonder: "Lord, I have heard from many about this man, how much harm he has done to Your saints in Jerusalem. And here he has authority from the chief priests to bind all who call on Your name" (Acts 9:13–14). Graciously, the Lord Jesus revealed His ultimate purpose while also reiterating His clear command: "Go," he told Ananias again, "for he is a chosen vessel of Mine to bear My name before Gentiles, kings, and the children of Israel" (Acts 9:15).

Understandably, Ananias had been concerned about the suffering that Saul had already caused and might well cause again. Jesus instead revealed to Ananias the suffering that Saul himself (known later as Paul) would undergo: "I will show him how many things he must suffer for My name's sake" (Acts 9:16).

Ananias did not argue, but simply obeyed: "Ananias went his way and entered the house; and laying his hands on him he said, 'Brother Saul, the Lord Jesus, who appeared to you on the road as you came, has sent me that you may receive your sight and be filled with the Holy Spirit" (Acts 9:17). Another life of incredible adventure had begun, all because Ananias was available.

In the next chapter we again see the command "Arise therefore...and go" (Acts 10:20), this time from the Holy Spirit to the apostle Peter, who was sent to take the gospel to Cornelius, a Gentile and a Roman centurion. Again there was immediate obedience: "Peter went" (Acts 10:23). Another available member of the Body of Christ went as he was instructed to another awakening soul, and another incredible adventure began.

Who had told Philip to go? Who told Ananias to go? Who told Peter to go?

The Lord Jesus, as Head of His body, the Church, redeemed sinners indwelt by His Spirit and available to Christ.

Who was running the Church in the book of Acts?

Not some committee or ecclesiastical hierarchy, but Jesus. The believers were put into action at His command; they were told to go, and they went. They knew what it meant to be a Christian, to become simply the suit of clothes that Jesus wears, so that the results would have only one possible explanation: Christ enthroned within the heart of every forgiven sinner.

This is the true Church in action, the right people in the right place at the right time saying the right things to the right people. The Church in action is where the Lord Jesus is still at work, clothed with the humanity of healthy members of His Body.

When you and I, in the discharge of our responsibility, share Jesus with others, we can have the hilarious expectation that something of timeless worth is happening, whether we fully see it or not.

It makes the Christian life so incredibly exciting!

We are ambassadors for Christ.

2 CORINTHIANS 5:20

→ Are you a healthy member of the Body of Christ, ready and willing to go where you are sent and to do as you are told?

→ Is your life filled with that which is of timeless worth?

→ Is your life the incredibly exciting adventure which God wants it to be?

The Main Thrust

aving come to a point in life of being entirely exhausted, Bonnie Hain had concluded that it simply was not worth the struggle to go on.

One day, anticipating that her husband would be late arriving home, Bonnie wrote him a note and left it on the kitchen table. It said, "I did it in the bathtub so you wouldn't have to clean up the mess."

In the providence of God, her husband came home early that day. He found his wife in the bathtub with both her wrists slit, but he arrived in time to save her life.

A PLEA IS ANSWERED

Bonnie and her husband were not Christians, nor did they have any understanding of what it really means to be a Christian. When they arrived home later from the hospital, however, Bonnie's husband placed a phone call to a local pastor he had never met. "Would you please come?" he pleaded. "It's an emergency."

The pastor, Bob Hobson, had once experienced his own

time of deep despair in his life and ministry, and it was during this time that I had known the joy of leading Bob to an understanding and appropriation of the indwelling Life of Christ.

Now, in response to this plea from a couple he did not know, Bob went to see them. He led them both to Christ, and he fully understood what that means. He did not just invite them to join his church or even simply to make a decision for Jesus so they could head toward heaven instead of hell. He led them to *Christ*. He invited them to receive *Somebody*, so that *Somebody* could live in them, Somebody living in somebody.

Such truth was revolutionary for this couple. From the moment of their genuine conversion, they fully grasped the implication of being born from above and becoming the recipients of the resurrection Life of the One who was crucified and then rose from the dead to share His Life with them on earth on their way to heaven. Life has held this same excitement for them ever since.

I have come to know Bonnie well, and I have often quoted a poem that she wrote three months after she came so close to dying by her own hand:

DISCOVERING...CHRIST IN ME!

Discovering daily who God really is,
   Thanking Him daily He's mine and I'm His,
Discovering daily God's great love for me;
   Such mercy, forgiveness, amazingly free.

Discovering daily that God really cares,
    Discovering daily He does answer prayers,
Discovering daily what grace really means:
    Unmerited favor beyond all my dreams.

Discovering daily God speaking to me;
    He speaks through the Bible. Once blind, now I see.
Discovering, discovering each day that I live
    That all that I need, He freely will give.

Discovering daily Christ working through me,
    Accomplishing daily what never could be.
Discovering daily: I can't, but He can;
    Thanking Him daily for my place in His plan.

Discovering daily how real life can be
    When I'm living in Christ and He's living in me.
Discovering daily a song in my heart
    With anticipation for each day to start.

Delighting and basking in love so divine,
    Secure in the knowledge I'm His and He's mine.
Besides mere contentment, excitement I see!
    A daily adventure: *Christ living in me!*

A FINAL REMINDER

As a closing encouragement for you to keep on track in your own daily adventure of "Christ living in me," allow me to

summarize this book's message.

Truth is as timeless as God Himself—it never changes. It may be forgotten, neglected, perverted, opposed, rejected, counterfeited, or displaced, but it never changes.

Truth is not an emphasis, a concept, a "party line," or merely an option. Truth is an imperative.

God created us in such a way that the presence of God as Creator within the human being as creature is imperative to our humanity. We, in normality, are to be distinguished from the animal kingdom by a quality of life and behavior that can have no possible explanation apart from God Himself indwelling us by His Holy Spirit.

This fact is *truth*. It is not subject to debate or dialogue. It is not an option to be offered, but a fact to be proclaimed. Truth does not evolve over the years any more than God evolves or Christ evolves.

INDISPENSABLE TO YOUR HUMANITY

In assuming our humanity, the Lord Jesus Christ chose to play the role of a human being as God intended man to be. The One by whom "all things were created" (Colossians 1:16) chose to *be* the kind of Man that He, as Creator, had made.

In declaring that He, as Man, could do nothing without the Father (John 5:19), Christ demonstrated the truth that has always been true—that we as human beings can do nothing without Him. In the same way that the Father, as God, was indispensable to Christ as Man in His life on earth, Christ as God is now indispensable to us as human beings in our lives.

To recognize and practice this truth is the nature of true repentance, and without this repentance there can be no true faith, for true repentance compels us to be totally dependent upon Christ as He was totally dependent upon the Father. Christ in us must do the work now as the Father in Him did the work then. In this way we let God "loose" in the world. God Himself becomes the ultimate limit, at His discretion, of what is possible.

THE HEART OF THE GOSPEL

This gives us an entirely new dimension to our understanding of the gospel and the remedial measures it proclaims. We come to understand not only that Christ died *for* us in the redemptive act, but that He rose again from the dead to live His Life *in* us, in the regenerative purpose of God.

It is through the resurrection of Christ that we are born again, just as the apostle Peter teaches us: "Blessed be the God and Father of our Lord Jesus Christ, who according to His abundant mercy has begotten us again to a living hope *through the resurrection of Jesus Christ* from the dead" (1 Peter 1:3). Paul therefore proclaimed that "if Christ is not risen, then our preaching is empty and your faith is also empty" (1 Corinthians 15:14). *The resurrection of Christ is at the very heart of the gospel!*

Any departure from this truth is a corruption of our

minds and has its origin in the subtlety of Satan. Aware of this danger, Paul expressed his utmost concern: "I fear, lest somehow, as the serpent deceived Eve by his craftiness, so your minds may be corrupted from the simplicity that is in Christ" (2 Corinthians 11:3).

FRUITFUL, AND SET FREE

This new birth which the resurrection of Christ makes possible is a divine conception with supernatural results. Just as a man takes a woman to be his wife so that his life, imparted to her, may be reproduced in and through her, so we too have been espoused to One Husband, Christ; that we "may be married…to Him who was raised from the dead, that we should bear fruit to God" (Romans 7:4). His life, imparted to us by the Holy Spirit at our new birth, is then reproduced in and through us, to "raise up the foundations of many generations" (Isaiah 58:12). We bear fruit that abides to His eternal praise.

The Lord Jesus Christ established the fact that our spiritual union with Him, like His own spiritual union with the Father, is the true and ultimate basis of all true evangelism, missions, and church planting. His prayer to His Father in John 17:21–23 was essentially this: "The world will know and the world will believe that You, the Father, have sent Me when My followers are in Us as I am in Thee, Father, and I am in them as Thou art in Me!"

The indwelling Life of Christ—that is the truth that sets us free!

Another Christian Classic

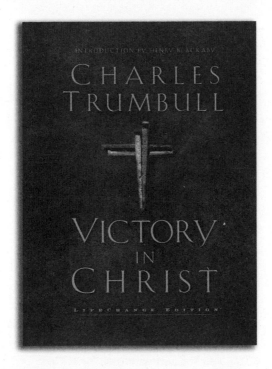

Christians have tremendous victory in Christ.
Embracing Him means ceasing to live by self-driven
efforts and, instead, completely surrendering to Christ.
The freedom that then ensues is God's gift of grace.

Victory in Christ
by Charles Trumbull
1-59052-254-0
US $9.99

Multnomah® Publishers *Keeping Your Trust…One Book at a Time®*